SpringerBriefs in Cybersecurity

Cybersecurity is a difficult and complex field. The technical, political and legal questions surrounding it are complicated, often stretching a spectrum of diverse technologies, varying legal bodies, different political ideas and responsibilities. Cybersecurity is intrinsically interdisciplinary, and most activities in one field immediately affect the others. Technologies and techniques, strategies and tactics, motives and ideologies, rules and laws, institutions and industries, power and money—all of these topics have a role to play in cybersecurity, and all of these are tightly interwoven.

The SpringerBriefs in Cybersecurity series is comprised of two types of briefs: topic- and country-specific briefs. Topic-specific briefs strive to provide a comprehensive coverage of the whole range of topics surrounding cybersecurity, combining whenever possible legal, ethical, social, political and technical issues. Authors with diverse backgrounds explain their motivation, their mindset, and their approach to the topic, to illuminate its theoretical foundations, the practical nuts and bolts and its past, present and future. Country-specific briefs cover national perceptions and strategies, with officials and national authorities explaining the background, the leading thoughts and interests behind the official statements, to foster a more informed international dialogue.

More information about this series at http://www.springer.com/series/10634

Lior Tabansky • Isaac Ben Israel

Cybersecurity in Israel

Springer

Lior Tabansky
The Blavatnik Interdisciplinary Cyber Research Center (ICRC)
Tel Aviv University
Tel Aviv, Israel

Isaac Ben Israel
The Blavatnik Interdisciplinary Cyber Research Center (ICRC)
Tel Aviv University
Tel Aviv, Israel

ISSN 2193-973X ISSN 2193-9748 (electronic)
SpringerBriefs in Cybersecurity
ISBN 978-3-319-18985-7 ISBN 978-3-319-18986-4 (eBook)
DOI 10.1007/978-3-319-18986-4

Library of Congress Control Number: 2015944077

Springer Cham Heidelberg New York Dordrecht London

Printed on acid-free paper

Springer International Publishing AG Switzerland is part of Springer Science+Business Media (www.springer.com)

Foreword

Lior Tabansky and Isaac Ben-Israel, a chief cyber-strategist for Israel's government, have compiled a wonderful piece of work. In their SpringerBrief *Cybersecurity in Israel*, they move with ease and elegance from theoretical and historical observations and insights in the field of strategic cybersecurity to the highly specific cases of cybersecurity in Israel – certainly one of the most challenging countries in security. Tabansky and Ben-Israel show that Israel has done a marvelous job in some of these areas. It is a small country, but well-resourced and certainly smart in security matters and, as such, provides a highly interesting case in cybersecurity.

This book successfully illustrates, explains, and analyzes this specific set of options and conditions in front of the larger backdrop of cybersecurity. Tabansky and Ben-Israel start with basic illustrations of Israel's security situation, from its "Tfisat HaBitachon," the National Security Concept, to more detailed descriptions of the Israeli innovation ecosystem and recent developments of Israel's cybersecurity policy. It includes fields of application such as the civil industry and e-Government and the more demanding cases of critical infrastructure protection and military cyber-defense, providing a unique look at Israel's offensive forces, their planning, and their perceptions. They finish with an analytical chapter recapitulating the strategic process, the lessons learned, the risks, and also the impact of national culture.

Tabansky's and Ben-Israel's SpringerBrief is an excellent achievement and a perfect fit for the series. It gives a very rich, interesting, and highly structured account and can be read as a narrative piece of technology and security history. It illustrates and provides an example in how to apply insights and options in cybersecurity to a more unique case. It entails so many inside views from processes and steps that theoreticians and practitioners alike will greatly enjoy this book and benefit from it.

I thank the authors for this great addition to our series. They provide great value.

April 2015

Sandro Gaycken
ESMT Berlin

Acknowledgments

This coauthored book results from the years spent conceptualizing, promoting, teaching, and debating the role of science and technology in international security. We are grateful to all counterparts we have spoken to in conferences, seminars, interviews, and task forces.

We are grateful to Tel Aviv University's Blavatnik Interdisciplinary Cyber Research Centre (ICRC) and the National Cyber Bureau for supporting this publication.

We are grateful to Tel Aviv University's Social Science Faculty, the Security Studies Program, and the Yuval Ne'eman Workshop for Science, Technology, and Security for the opportunity to pursue new cross-disciplinary research directions.

We thank the indispensable Ms. Revital Yaron, who has been foreseeing administrative problems and solving them.

We thank our colleagues who have helped develop the ideas, especially Mr. Niv David and Adv. Deborah Housen-Couriel of the Yuval Ne'eman Workshop who critically read the manuscript.

Acknowledgements

List of Abbreviations and Glossary

BERD	Business Expenditure on Research and Development
BGU	Ben-Gurion University of the Negev
BIU	Bar Ilan University
CEO	Chief Executive Officer
CERT-IL	Israel National Cyber Event Readiness Team
CHE (מל"ג)	Council of Higher Education
CI	Critical Infrastructures
CIA	Confidentiality, Integrity, and Availability
CIP	Critical Infrastructure Protection
CSIS	Center for Strategic and International Studies
DDoS	Distributed Denial-of-Service Attack
DDR&D	(*Maf'at* מפא"ת) Ministry of Defense Directorate for Research and Development
DoD	US Department of Defense
ENISA	European Network and Information Security Agency
ERP	Enterprise Resource Planning Management Software
EU	European Union
FP7 EU's	Seventh Framework Programme
GDE	Gross Domestic Expenditure
GDP	Gross Domestic Product
HMI	Human–Machine Interface
HPC	High-Performance Computer
HR	Human Resources
HUJI	Hebrew University of Jerusalem
IAEA	International Atomic Energy Agency
IAF	Israeli Air Force
I-CORE	Israeli Centres of Research Excellence
ICRC	The Tel Aviv University Blavatnik Interdisciplinary Cyber Research Centre
ICT	Information and Communication Technologies
IDF	(*Tzahal* צה"ל) Israeli Defence Forces

IEC	Israel Electric Company
ILITA	*(Ramot רמו"ט)* Israeli Law, Information, and Technology Authority
INCB	Israel National Cyber Bureau
INSS	Institute for National Security Studies
ISA	(*Shabak* שב"כ) Israel Security Agency
ISAC	Information Sharing and Analysis Centres
IT	Information Technology
IT-RMA	Information Technology Revolution in Military Affairs
NCRD	*(Molmop מולמ"פ)* National Council for Research and Development, Ministry of Science, Technology and Space
NCSA	(*Rashut Le'umit le-Haganat ha-Cyber* רשות לאומית להגנת הסייבר) National Cyber Security Authority
NISA	(*Re'em*) National Information Security Authority
NPT	Nuclear Non-Proliferation Treaty
NSC	(מל"ל) National Security Council
OECD	Organisation for Economic Co-operation and Development
PBC	*(Vatat ות"ת)* Planning and Budgeting Committee of the Council of Higher Education
PLC	Programmable Logic Controller
PM	Prime Minister
PPP	Public–Private Partnerships
R&D	Research and Development
SCADA	Supervisory Control and Data Acquisition
TASE	Tel Aviv Stock Exchange
TAU	Tel Aviv University
TTC	Technology Transfer Company of a University
US	United States
VC	Venture Capital
WIS	Weizmann Institute of Science
YNW	Tel Aviv University Yuval Ne'eman Workshop for Science, Technology, and Security

Contents

Chapter 1
Introduction

Abstract This SpringerBrief introduces and analyses over two decades of Israeli cybersecurity policy. We discuss cybersecurity's complementary aspects and present the major risk that drives cybersecurity policies. We outline the issues and topics covered, sources used, and the research challenges. The analysis requires a broad strategic perspective as factors less tangible than technology such as culture and grand strategy influence the national cybersecurity. Finally, we present the book's scope and structure.

Keywords Israel • National strategy • Cybersecurity • Cyberpower • Information assurance • IT-security • Critical infrastructure

1.1 Introduction

Information and Communication Technologies (ICT) evolve at an exponential pace, as predicted and described by Moore's Law in 1965. This tempo of technological change is the driving force behind profound productivity, and economic and social change. Almost all aspects of life in modern society intertwine people with computing and communications. Generally, the 'cyber' prefix stands for electronic and computer related activities. Cyberspace is an elusive concept, usefully described as a global man-made *substrate*, with the Internet and the WWW as parts of it (Demchak 2011).

Enabled by information technology, the challenges of developing cyberspace are global. However, the responses to these changes, cybersecurity included, are local: they derive from the socio-political structure in which sovereign states are the main actors responsible for their citizens' security in the anarchic international system.

The resulting development of various national cybersecurity perspectives and policies is covered by this dedicated Springer series. This SpringerBrief introduces and analyses two decades of Israeli cybersecurity policy; we discuss the conceptual cybersecurity issues and the country-specific characteristics.

L. Tabansky, I. Ben Israel, *Cybersecurity in Israel*, SpringerBriefs in Cybersecurity, DOI 10.1007/978-3-319-18986-4_1

1.2 Cybersecurity: Making Sense of Complementing Perspectives

Cybersecurity issues arise because of a combination of three factors: the growing dependence on IT for societal functions; the human characteristics that lead to crime and war; and vulnerabilities in IT open to exploitation or that simply cause malfunction.

This brief views cybersecurity from an integrative national perspective. We see cybersecurity as a set of policies and actions with two interconnected goals: mitigating security *risks* and increasing resilience on the one hand, and leveraging *opportunities* enabled by the developing cyberspace on the other. To understand cybersecurity in a comprehensive, interdisciplinary manner is challenging. A combination of IT-security, military cyber-defence, intelligence, scientific research, technological development, education and human capital, entrepreneurship, and sectoral or organisational practices together compose national cybersecurity.

Among the complementing cybersecurity perspectives are technical IT-security, information Confidentiality, Integrity, and Availability (the CIA triad), cyber-war and military operations, homeland security, espionage, surveillance, civil liberties and privacy, information operations, security economics, risk-management, criminal, law-enforcement, and legal ones. Technical IT-security still is the predominant perspective in current cybersecurity literature.

However, IT-security is *not* cybersecurity, but rather one important technical aspect of it. Cybersecurity is about technologies, processes, and policies intended to prevent and reduce the negative impact of events in cyberspace, including those that are the result of deliberate actions against information technology by a hostile or malevolent actor (Council 2014, 1665). It is a live, dynamic, evolving set of processes, with pronounced variations across geographic, organisational, and temporal axes. The inadequacy of strictly technical perspectives is increasingly apparent.

1.2.1 The Main Cyber-Risks

Various developing cyber-risks have been surveyed and conceptually analysed, predominantly in the US (Brenner 2011; Deibert 2013; Kello 2013; Libicki 2007; Lindsay 2013; Lynn III 2010; Nye 2010; Peterson 2013; Rid 2013; Tabansky 2011, 2012). Following the spread of ITs, by the mid-1990s much of modern society had come to implement computerised control systems. Societies relied on a spectrum of interdependent, complex systems before the information revolution. Critical infrastructures affect all areas of a citizen's life in a modern society, but in the information age, computerised systems control the infrastructure, fusing the characteristics of information with the physical world. The added computerised information layer became indispensable for the proper functioning of society; the benefits are clear: increased efficiency, cost effectiveness, and new possibilities have brought unprecedented welfare. But the cyber-physical convergence also increases the potential physical damage from cyber-malfunctions and cyberattacks.

The characteristics of information and the current properties of cyberspace challenge centuries-old strategic axioms; specifically, the cyber-risk to civilian infrastructure is a revolutionary development in strategic affairs. Cyberspace allows a direct strike on national infrastructure without being physically present at or even in proximity to the location of the target. This allows the attacker to act without exposure or distinct attribution, or the risk of confronting actual armed defenders. Cyberattack circumvents traditional defence systems—this poses a strategic risk on both the national and international levels.

With increased recognition of the change and the risks involved, corporate and national cybersecurity policies started emerging in the 1990s, integrating the subsequently evolving nomenclature.

1.3 Strategic Aspects of Cybersecurity and Cyberpower

Presently, cybertechnology is becoming part of the deliberate effort to harness political, military, diplomatic, and economic tools to advance each nation's interests. Cyberpower is 'the ability to use cyberspace to create advantages and influence events in other operational environments and across the instruments of power' (Kuehl 2009, 184). Power, war, attack and deterrence have been a central part of human history. Security Studies is a relatively new discipline within the field of International Relations that studies the interplay of war, society and technology. If cyber-technology has any relevance to international security, then the rich scholarship of War and International Relations should not be overlooked (Farrell 2010; Gat 2006; Gilpin 1984). The popular habit of labelling any malicious action identified in the network or endpoint as a 'cyberattack' ignores the historical connotations of that term. The propensity to see 'cyber-threats' as malignant lines of code in passive machines ignores the people and organisations who utilise them, and their motives for doing so. The debate on cyber-war continues (Clarke and Knake 2010, 84; Rid 2013, 442), while International Relations (IR) scholars at last begin to pay more attention to cybersecurity (Rid and Buchanan 2014, 1743; Eriksson and Giacomello 2014, 1774; Conway 2014, 1619; Axelrod and Iliev 2014, 1463; Lindsay 2013, 1055; Kello 2013, 1326; Junio 2013, 1327; Deibert 2013, 999; Betz and Stevens 2013, 938; Liff 2012, 435; Betz 2012, 1635).

Over time, the word 'strategy' lost its meaning through ubiquitous overuse. The term originated in the ancient Greek context of armed conflict. A workable definition is found in Sir Lawrence Freedman's recent book, *Strategy: A History*: 'Strategy is about getting more out of a situation than the starting balance of power would suggest. It is the art of creating power' (2013, 1808). When adopting this definition of strategy, the potential of cyberspace to alter the balance of power becomes easier to grasp.

The British military historian, Sir Basil Liddell Hart, popularised the term grand strategy during the mid-twentieth century in the context of war. Subsequent definitions of grand strategy are based on his insight that it involves synchronising means and political, military, diplomatic and economic tools to achieve the highest level of national policy to advance that state's national interest.

The global reach of information technology and the Internet notwithstanding, any state strives to use cyberspace for national interests. Indeed, states develop capabilities that they deem necessary and feasible (Lewis et al. 2013). It is increasingly recognised that states have different perspectives on and approaches to cyberspace in general and cybersecurity in particular, as featured in this Springer series.

1.4 Scope and Limitations

This SpringerBrief's focus on the national policy level acknowledges that a multitude of information, security initiatives, standards, and developments in various business sectors stand beyond its scope. Furthermore, the focus on policy limits discussing fascinating scientific developments arising in this fast-moving environment. The absence of an in-depth discussion on these topics is not due to their insignificance but because they reach beyond this book's field of reference.

With defence and intelligence agencies traditionally acting as major stakeholders in cyber-defence, many sources are classified. This presents obstacles for a public researcher, as the defence and intelligence communities' role in early and present-day cybersecurity is largely inaccessible. That said, the defence and intelligence perspective is only one among others, including CIP, homeland security, the balance between basic freedoms and security needs, IT-security, espionage, crime, and information attacks. Often these perspectives are more important than the military one. Therefore, the attention given to direct defence and intelligence roles in this study is limited.

Researching national cybersecurity is probably harder in Israel than in many other democracies. Observers are often surprised by the fact that Israel has not published a formal, public national strategy document—such as the French *Le Livre Blanc sur la Défense et la Sécurité Nationale* or the American *Quadrennial Defense Review*—in decades. Even with the volatile geo-political environment, ever-changing threats, new opportunities, and the resulting dynamism throughout the Israeli defence establishment, national leadership avoids publishing declarative documents. However, throughout history, rarely do we find an orderly movement to advanced-set goals; strategy emerges as fluid and flexible (Freedman 2013, 1785). Organisations and individuals respond to challenges without a centralized and clear decision-making process. While often not reflected in periodical official publications, the Israeli defence and political establishments adapt dynamically to the volatile geo-political environment.

1.4.1 Sources for the Israeli Case

This SpringerBrief utilises the few official documents and reputable periodicals publicly available. Most importantly, it benefits from co-author Isaac Ben-Israel's long-lasting involvement in the national cyber-policy efforts, and first-hand experience advising top-level Israeli government entities. Moreover, the co-authors' experience in developing and hosting the pioneering Public-Private Partnerships (PPP) via the Tel Aviv University (TAU) Yuval Ne'eman Workshop for Science, Technology, and Security (YNW) provides invaluable personal exchanges with the key stakeholders throughout the business, academia, government and defence sectors.[1] This SpringerBrief further draws from the systematic interdisciplinary academic approach to cybersecurity, developed by the authors in the Blavatnik Interdisciplinary Cyber Research Center (ICRC) at Tel Aviv University.

1.5 Structure

The SpringerBrief's focus on national policy level of cybersecurity is fitting since security is the main duty of the state, and the anarchic international system imposes costs for states neglecting national security. The most straightforward approach to present a national perspective coherently is to use a historical sequence, and then subject the whole story to analysis. Therefore, this SpringerBrief holds several sections:

Chapter 2 outlines the *Tfisat HaBitachon* (National Security Concept) – the grand strategy Israel developed, implemented, and maintains security to counter the harsh geopolitical environment in which the state exists.

Chapter 3 delves into the Israeli innovation ecosystem. We discuss the roles of universities, IDF-service, defence, government and business R&D, in innovation and human capital development. The cultural traits enable the institutions. We emphasise the Israeli innovation ecosystem roots that stem from the grand strategy. Having laid out the appropriate analytical context, we proceed to present the case study.

Chapters 4, 5, 6, 7, 8, and 9 outline the historical-evolutionary development of Israeli cybersecurity in a chronological order. We discuss the stakeholders' encounters with the inevitable cybersecurity dilemmas and describe the policy-making processes.

Chapter 4 describes the 1995–2002 early sporadic response to the newly apparent cyberspace risks and opportunities. Followed by several defence leaders recognising the exponential potentials of technological progress, Israeli IT-security, and e-Government efforts took shape.

Chapter 5 presents and analyses the unique Critical Infrastructure Protection (CIP) arrangement instated in Israel in 2002. It was one of the first national cybersecurity policies in the world.

Chapter 6 discusses the further efforts to develop national cybersecurity policy, looking beyond IT-security in the critical infrastructure and defence sectors. Israel's prime minister undertook the National Cyber Initiative by administering

[1] Given the understandable delicateness of the subject, we purposely refrain from attributing opinions and positions to persons, offices or companies throughout the book.

an external multi-stakeholder taskforce, and pursued a comprehensive approach to cybersecurity as part of the national cyber-strategy. The National Cyber Initiative report, produced by an external team of experts headed by Professor Ben-Israel, laid the foundation for the 2011 Israeli Cyber-strategy.[2]

Chapter 7 examines the now de-facto national cyber-strategy of Israel that stemmed from the National Cyber Initiative. The national cyber-strategy also explores cyberspace's macro-economic and strategic benefits for Israel in the international arena while striving to increase cybersecurity. The Israel National Cyber Bureau (INCB) was established to coordinate and foster the national cyber-policy effort; we discuss its actions.

Chapter 8 addresses the recent (2014–2015) steps in Israeli cybersecurity policy evolution: we present background and policy design leading to establishing the National Cyber Security Authority (NCSA) and the emerging rearrangement of responsibility. The Israeli national cybersecurity posture is changing again driven by important non-technical aspects.

Chapter 9 presents the cybersecurity developments in the Israeli Defence Forces (IDF): human capital development, and doctrinal views. Operation Orchard and Stuxnet, the cyberattacks attributed to Israel by foreign sources, illustrate effectiveness, attribution, and deterrence challenges. Cyber-warfare suits Israeli grand strategy, but military capacity is only one element of national cybersecurity.

Chapter 10 recapitulates the general conclusions presented and discussed throughout the book: the complementing aspects of cybersecurity; the major risk that drives policies; the strategic background, and the distinctive phases in the evolution of cybersecurity policy in Israel. We reiterate that the often overlooked national culture and grand strategy crucially influence cybersecurity policy and practice.

1.6 Conclusion

The analysis of national cybersecurity requires a broad strategic perspective. This SpringerBrief on Israeli cybersecurity integrates the historical sequence of key events, actors, policies and milestones into the strategic backdrop. The following Chaps. 2 and 3 provide the essential analytical background on the Israeli grand strategy and the Israeli innovation ecosystem. Chapters 4, 5, 6, 7, 8 and 9 present the distinctive phases in the evolution of cybersecurity policy in Israel, and Chap. 10 recapitulates the Israeli experience to enhance fruitful policy efforts in likeminded countries.

---

[2] Ben-Israel is the co-author of this SpringerBrief.

References

Axelrod R, Iliev R (2014) Timing of cyber conflict. Proc Natl Acad Sci 111(4):1298–1303

Betz D (2012) Cyberpower in strategic affairs: neither unthinkable nor blessed. J Strateg Stud 35(5):689–711. doi:10.1080/01402390.2012.706970

Betz DJ, Stevens T (2013) Analogical reasoning and cyber security. Secur Dialogue 44(2):147–164. doi:10.1177/0967010613478323

Brenner J (2011) America the vulnerable: inside the new threat matrix of digital espionage, crime, and warfare. Penguin, New York

Clarke RA, Knake RK (2010) Cyber war: the next threat to national security and what to do about it. Ecco, New York

Conway M (2014) Reality check: assessing the (un)likelihood of cyberterrorism. In: Chen TM, Jarvis L, Macdonald S (eds) Cyberterrorism. Springer, New York, pp 103–121

Council NR (2014) At the nexus of cybersecurity and public policy: some basic concepts and issues (Clark D, Berson T, Lin HS, eds). p 150. Retrieved from catalog/18749/at-the-nexus-ofcybersecurity-and-public-policy-some-basic

Deibert RJ (2013) Black code: inside the battle for cyberspace. McClelland & Stewart, Toronto

Demchak CC (2011) Wars of disruption and resilience cybered conflict, power, and national security. The University of Georgia Press, Athens/London

Eriksson J, Giacomello G (2014) International relations, cybersecurity, and content analysis: a constructivist approach. In: The global politics of science and technology, vol 2. Springer, New York, pp 205–219

Farrell T (2010) Security studies: critical concepts in international relations. Routledge, Milton Park/Abingdon/New York

Freedman L (2013) Strategy: a history. Oxford University Press, Oxford

Gat A (2006) War in human civilization. Oxford University Press, Oxford/New York

Gilpin RG (1984) The richness of the tradition of political realism. Int Org 38(02):287–304. doi:10.1017/S0020818300026710

Junio TJ (2013) How probable is cyber war? Bringing IR theory back in to the cyber conflict debate. J Strateg Stud 36(1):125–133. doi:10.1080/01402390.2012.739561

Kello L (2013) The meaning of the cyber revolution: perils to theory and statecraft. Int Secur 38(2):7–40. doi:10.1162/ISEC_a_00138

Kuehl DT (2009) Cyberspace and cyberpower. In: Kramer FD, Starr SH, Wentz LK (eds) Cyberpower and national security. National Defense University Press/Potomac Books, Washington, DC

Lewis JA, Neuneck G, United Nations Institute for Disarmament Research, Center for Strategic and International Studies, Universität, H, Institut für Friedensforschung und, S (2013) The cyber index: international security trends and realities

Libicki MC (2007) Conquest in cyberspace: national security and information warfare. Cambridge University Press, New York

Liff AP (2012) Cyberwar: a new absolute weapon? The proliferation of cyberwarfare capabilities and interstate war. J Strateg Stud 1–28

Lindsay JR (2013) Stuxnet and the limits of cyber warfare. Secur Stud 22(3):365–404. doi:10.1080/09636412.2013.816122

Lynn WJ III (2010) Defending a new domain the Pentagon's cyberstrategy. [Article]. Foreign Aff 89(5):97

Nye JS (2010) Cyber power: Belfer Center for Science and International Affairs. Harvard Kennedy School, Cambridge

Peterson D (2013) Offensive cyber weapons: construction, development, and employment. J Strateg Stud 36(1):120–124

Rid T (2013) Cyber war will not take place. Hurst, London
Rid T, Buchanan B (2014) Attributing cyber attacks. J Strateg Stud 1–34. doi:10.1080/01402390.2014.977382
Tabansky L (2011) Basic concepts in cyber warfare. Mil Strateg Aff 3(1):75–92
Tabansky L (2012) Cybercrime: a national security issue? Mil Strateg Aff 4(3):117–136

Chapter 2
Geopolitics and Israeli Strategy

Abstract This chapter presents *Tfisat HaBitachon*, the National Security Concept: the grand strategy that Israel has developed to fulfil the vision of its Zionist founders in the harsh geopolitical environment. We discuss the lasting role of science and technology in Israeli national security. The conscious thrust towards qualitative superiority, including harnessing IT, remains the central aspect of the Israeli grand strategy. The Israeli cybersecurity perspective, capabilities and policy have their roots in this grand strategy.

Keywords National security concept • Grand strategy • Cybersecurity • Arab-Israeli conflict • 'Iron Wall' • Quality • Qualitative superiority

2.1 Israeli Grand Strategy Drives Cybersecurity

National cybersecurity policy has two interconnected goals: mitigating security *risks* and leveraging *opportunities*. Naturally, states' perspectives, goals, means, environment and strategies vary.

Israel's national security environment has always been extraordinarily volatile, uncertain and extreme due to the contested location of the Land of Israel in the Arab-Muslim Middle East. Already in 1920, the *Yishuv*—pre-State Jewish community during British Mandate—was attacked in massive Arab riots.[1] The following 1929 riots and the 1936 Arab Revolt met with the immediate establishment of Jewish defence forces. Then in 1948, the War of Independence broke out, threatening the survival of the Jewish population in newly founded State of Israel. Israel has engaged in several consequential wars, reached peace agreements with neighbouring Egypt (1979) and Jordan (1994), and withstood waves of Palestinian and Islamic terrorism.

Despite these great strides, the geopolitical situation remains unstable. The existential threat posed by the aspiring nuclear Islamic Republic of Iran is looming. The implosion of what remained of the colonial Sykes-Picot (1916) political order

[1] Interestingly these riots started by what remains a recurring theme: false rumours that the Jews planned to build a synagogue on the Temple Mount in Jerusalem.

L. Tabansky, I. Ben Israel, *Cybersecurity in Israel*, SpringerBriefs in Cybersecurity, DOI 10.1007/978-3-319-18986-4_2

in the Middle East; disassembling Syria, Iraq and other countries along sectarian lines and the rise of global Jihadist non-state organisations may well present new security challenges for Israel. How, then, has Israel become a prosperous, vibrant, open, society with an innovative economy,[2] and a proud member of the developed Western world while facing these ongoing threats?

2.2 Israeli Grand Strategy

The Zionist movement emerged with modern nationalism in nineteenth-century Europe, seeking through self-determination the establishment of a Jewish democratic state in the Land of Israel, and the ingathering of the remaining Jewish Diaspora to it. Israel's significant geopolitical inferiority in the region concerned the thinkers and political leaders of the Zionist movement since the early twentieth century. Ze'ev Jabotinsky's Iron Wall concept is a prominent example of Israeli grand strategy in light of the geopolitical constraint. Anticipating the native Arab population's resistance to sharing the land with Zionist Jewish immigrants, Jabotinsky (1923) outlined the Zionist response:

> We must either suspend our settlement efforts or continue them without paying attention to the mood of the natives. Settlement can thus develop under the protection of a force that is not dependent on the local population, behind an iron wall, which they will be powerless to breach. (*The Iron Wall*: *We and the Arabs* 1923)

A peaceful coexistence between Arabs and Jews would be possible in the distant future, but only because of erecting an impregnable wall:

> It is my hope and belief that we will then offer them guarantees that will satisfy them and that both peoples will live in peace as good neighbours. But the sole way to such an agreement is through the iron wall, that is to say, the establishment in Palestine of a force that will in no way be influenced by Arab pressure. (Jabotinsky 1923)

Despite the conflicting political ideologies within the *Yishuv*, there was a consensus regarding the need for a strong defence given the stark imbalance of power. David Ben-Gurion (1886–1973), the builder of the *Yishuv*'s political and military power and the architect behind the modern State of Israel, concluded that the conflict with the Arabs was inescapable. Ben-Gurion formulated a pragmatic strategy starting after the Arab Revolt of 1936, which is similar to the 'Iron Wall' of his political opponent, (Jabotinsky 1923; Ben-Israel 2013 #1808; Shlaim 2001 #1650). In late 1948, the starting points in shaping Ben-Gurion's outlook on military organization after the war were, on the one hand, that even after the fighting ceases and peace prevails, Israel will need to maintain "*consistent and efficient preparedness for defense at any time*," and on the other hand, that Israel is economically unable to sustain a large regular army, especially in light of the state's expected reprioritization

---

[2] Since 1948, the Israeli population has grown 11-fold; GDP per capita grew from $2000 to $33000.

with its emphasis on absorption of new immigrants and development of the country through settlement, construction of infrastructure, and economic growth. Ben-Gurion's goal was to successfully combine the operationalization and growth of the economy with the development of a military defense capability. In order to achieve this goal he insisted on the need to provide the armed forces with the following:

> The best and most advanced training and proper military equipment, so that the superior quality of the armed forces will compensate for its inferior quantity, and if at the same time we succeed in training all members of the nation who are of an age to bear arms and train them to stand guard without too much disruption to their ongoing work within the economy. Only through these two [means]—training the *entire nation* for effective defense and providing advanced and *superior training and equipment* to the defenders—can we ensure effective military preparedness for the defense of the State of Israel. (Shlaim 2001)

The Israeli grand strategy included the following elements to minimise the risks of war in this harsh geopolitical climate:

- The quest for qualitative superiority to balance numerical inferiority
- An emphasis on intelligence for early warning, due to total lack of strategic depth and numerical inferiority
- An emphasis on deterrence to prevent a catastrophic war, including early investment in nuclear research
- An alliance with a global superpower to increase deterrence, strengthen the "Iron Wall" and restrain the neighbours' appetite for an all-out attack
- The quest for decisive victory: If or when hostilities break out, offensive tactics designed to achieve a decisive victory on the battlefield are preferred. This maxim also led to developing a unique deterrence posture (Ben-Israel 2013; Rid 2012).

2.3 The Role of Science

Prior to creating the modern State of Israel in 1948, the Jewish leaders realised that a poor country without natural resources would only have a chance of succeeding if it invested massively in its human capital via education, science, and technology. In 1901, the fifth Zionist Congress called for the establishment of a Jewish university in Palestine—a territory governed by the Ottoman Empire—that led to the founding of two universities—the Technion in Haifa (1912) and the Hebrew University in Jerusalem (1925). After creating the independent State of Israel, David Ben-Gurion, its first prime minister, prioritised strengthening its major universities and establishing more advanced research centres, including the special Science Force within *Tzahal* (the Israeli Defence Forces), later transformed to RAFAEL and new defence industries (Haan 2011).

2.4 A Qualitative Edge

The Israeli national security concept must balance its numerical inferiority. The concept of qualitative superiority, based in science and technology in particular, has been perceived from the early days of Israel as a central factor in the power equation between Israel and its neighbours.

This explicitly includes the education provided to citizens, the scientific infrastructure, the continuing emphasis on research and development, the quality of weapons systems, the art of war, morale, and motivation among the armed forces, as well as economic development. In this spirit, Ben-Gurion strived to gather the best scientific powers the Jewish people have to offer and adapt their actions to the security needs and development of the country.

Developing and maintaining a qualitative edge in all civilian and military realms is a ceaseless endeavour. Thus, Israel invested exceptional resources in acquiring the latest scientific and technological capabilities from its early—and very poor—years, and has since sustained significant efforts to promote basic scientific research and applied defence technology (Peres 1970). The strategy manifests primarily in countering the changing national security threats on technical, tactical, operational, and strategic levels. We argue that the macro-economic policy also reflects the same grand strategy.

2.4.1 IT in National Security: Intelligence, RMA, and Counter-Terrorism

The intelligence services are pivotal in developing and fielding unique technological solutions to fulfil their demanding mission. Intelligence plays a key role in the Israeli security concept due to the lack of strategic depth,[3] and the technology-intensive missions of the intelligence agencies and the air force has driven continuous investment in IT. Developing IT has led to a wave of thinking concerning the effect of technologies on security. Information Technology Revolution in Military Affairs (IT-RMA) was an American concept prescribing information dominance, intelligence, effective long-range precision strikes and dominant manoeuvre, all enabled by IT and satellites, as demonstrated by the US military in the 1991 Operation Desert Storm and in further operations. The operational success exceeded planners' expectations, and it became the model for IT-RMA: A smart, advanced, agile force efficiently prevailing against a larger armoured army.

In parallel to, and sometimes preceding the American developments, *Tzahal* (IDF) adopted, adapted, and assimilated the IT-RMA concept into the Israeli

[3] Strategic depth is a term in military literature that broadly refers to the distances between the front lines and the key centers of population.

strategy thanks to the IDF's relative openness to consider and experiment with emerging technology (Adamsky 2010). Throughout the IDF, IT proved instrumental in countering emerging threats.

The suicide bombers' 'intifada' violently took the lives of over a thousand Israeli civilians in 2000–2005, and caused a prolonged political, social, and economic crisis. Western-style defence forces appeared helpless against suicide attacks, while media maximised the terror effect. However, driven by its grand strategy, Israel commissioned its qualitative edge to counter the threat. By using high technology to produce real-time intelligence, IDF and *Shabaq* gradually gained the capability to carry out rapid targeted preventive operations. This qualitative superiority enabled the Israeli security forces to effectively disrupt the operations of terrorist organisations without massive land manoeuvres—that would have led to collateral damage unacceptable to Israel (Ben-Israel et al. 2006; Tabansky 2007). Aided by IT, Israel eventually restored security to the home front and subdued suicide terrorism. Using IT enabled information dominance and precision strikes in a manner otherwise impossible. This modus operandi remains valid to this day, as information dominance and a rapid surgical response counter modern hybrid threats.

2.5 Conclusion

We presented the national security concept—the grand strategy Israel has developed to balance geopolitical inferiority. The central element in the grand strategy is the quest towards achieving and maintaining a qualitative edge. Cyber Technology suits the Israeli national security concept: developing and implementing innovative technology-intensive (rather than labor-intensive) tools provides for a qualitative advantage.

However, a desire for advantage alone does not lead to success. A strategy, that involves setting goals, developing capabilities to achieve the goals, and mobilising resources to execute the actions- is necessary.

References

Adamsky D (2010) The culture of military innovation: the impact of cultural factors on the Revolution in Military Affairs in Russia, the U.S., and Israel. Stanford University Press, Stanford

Ben-Israel I (2013) Tefisat ha-bitahon shel Yisrael = Israel defence doctrine

Ben-Israel I, Setter O, Tishler A (2006) R&D and the war on terrorism: generalizing the Israeli experience. NATO Sci Ser V Sci Technol Policy 51:51–63

Haan U. d (2011) The Israel case of science and technology based entrepreneurship: an exploration cluster. In Mian SA (ed) Science and technology based regional entrepreneurship global experience in policy and program development. Edward Elgar Publishing, Inc, Cheltenham, UK. http://www.elgaronline.com/view/9781847203908.00021.xml

Jabotinsky Z (1923) The iron wall. The Jewish Herald, 6 November 1937
Peres S (1970) David's sling. Weidenfeld & Nicolson, London
Rid T (2012) Deterrence beyond the state: the Israeli experience. Contemp Secur Policy Contemp Secur Policy 33(1):124–147
Shlaim A (2001) The iron wall: Israel and the Arab world: WW Norton & Company
Tabansky L (2007) The anti-terrorism struggle in the information age: Palestinian suicide bombers and the implementation of high technologies in Israel's response, 2000–2005. (M.A.), TAU, Tel Aviv. Retrieved from http://bit.ly/cfzbFK

Chapter 3
The National Innovation Ecosystem of Israel

Abstract We concisely present the current Israeli innovation ecosystem to provide the required background for the description and analysis of Israeli national cybersecurity. National cybersecurity policies and specific national conditions are necessarily intertwined. Israeli national cybersecurity is best understood in context of the Israeli grand strategy.

The unique national innovation ecosystem Israel has been developing even prior to national independence, originates from the strategic principle of quality over quantity. The ecosystem is now comprised of the IDF service, domestic and foreign business R&D, defence R&D, public research universities, and government agencies. It is characterised by close geographical and institutional proximity, and by relative independence of the participating actors. The Israeli culture that encourages initiative, resourcefulness, and experimentation complements the institutional mechanisms.

Keywords Innovation • Ecosystem • Science • R&D policy • Tel Aviv University • IDF • R&D expenditure • GERD • BERD • H2020 • FP7 • Office of the Chief Scientist OCS • *Maf'at* • *Talpiot* • *Atuda* • *Yozma* • Venture Capital • CyberSpark • CyberGym

3.1 Israeli Grand Strategy Drives the Innovation Ecosystem

Israel is one of the global leaders in Hi-Tech, namely – computer science, electronics, and information technologies – the most tangible components of cybersecurity technology. But how did Israel get to the leadership position?

In the scope of this SpringerBrief, we stress the elaborate innovation ecosystem developed for achieving survival and strategic national goals. Innovation refers to new ways of accomplishing a task (Cheung et al. 2014). The academic innovation studies thrive in recent decades, most notably across economics, business management, political economy, technology and engineering (Lundvall 2010; Nelson 1993; Taylor 2012). The National Innovation System concept refers to all the interacting social and political factors inside a country that affect the creation and diffusion of innovation: culture, education, research institutions, credit system, fiscal policies, government incentives, law and intellectual right protection, political structure,

L. Tabansky, I. Ben Israel, *Cybersecurity in Israel*, SpringerBriefs in Cybersecurity, DOI 10.1007/978-3-319-18986-4_3

market conditions and so on. However, the study of defence innovation – the transformation of ideas and knowledge into new or improved products, processes and services for defence and dual-use purposes – has been largely compartmentalized (Grissom 2006). Further development and application of defence innovation framework, which exceeds the scope of this SpringerBrief, will contribute to the nascent cybersecurity studies.

Israel's innovation ecosystem is the outcome of its grand strategy as discussed in Chap. 2, geared for qualitative advantage to enhance national viability and security in the challenging geopolitical conditions. This ecosystem, ingrained in the cultural characteristics, creates the conditions for developing skilled, innovative human capital and cutting-edge science and technology throughout Israel (Fig. 3.1).

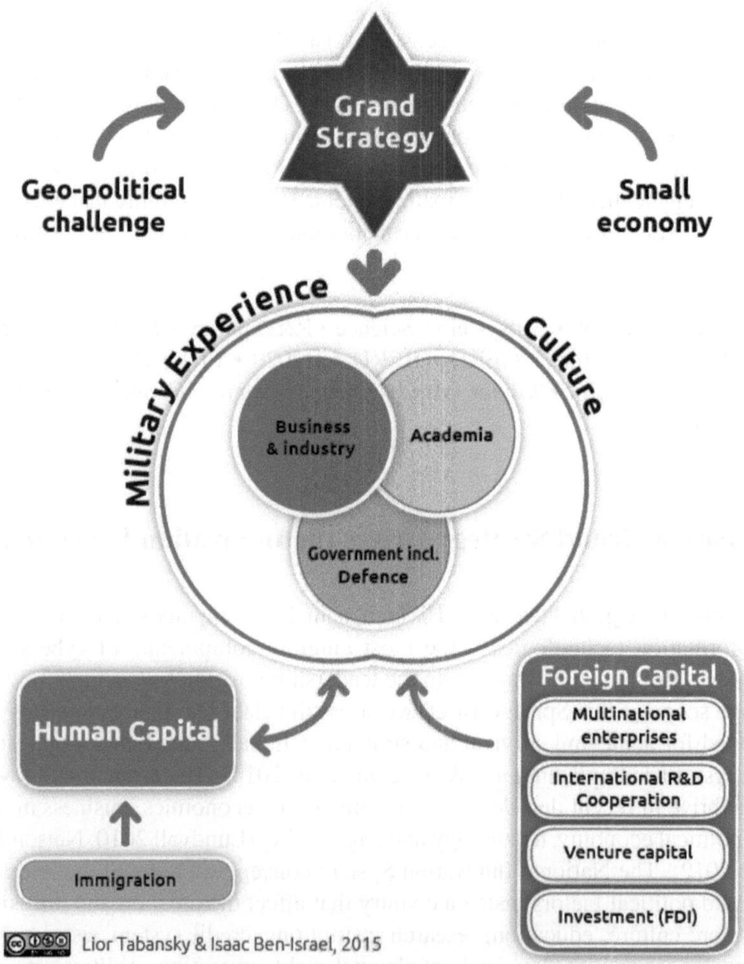

Fig. 3.1 Israel: national innovation ecosystem originates from the grand strategy

3.2 Performance Indicators

In the last 15 years, Israel's gross domestic expenditure on R&D has increased from 2.3 % in 1991 to 3.5 % in 1999 to 4.2 % of gross domestic product (GDP) in 2012. It is the highest share in the world, roughly *double* the Organisation for Economic Co-operation and Development (OECD) average (Fig. 3.2). Israel sustains this extraordinarily high rate of R&D expenditure despite the geopolitical challenges, and the resulting defence expenditure circa 6–8 % of the GDP.

Israel's main strengths are its human capital,[1] research infrastructure and high research intensity.[2] Israel has become one of the global innovation centres. From 148 countries, the World Economic Forum Global Competitiveness Report 2013–2014 ranks Israel 3rd in innovation, 6th in patent volume, and 8th in the ease of access to venture capital (VC); the quality of scientific research institutions in Israel is considered to be the best in the world (Schwab 2013). Business Expenditure on R&D (BERD) as a share of GDP is around 80 % – the second highest in the OECD arena; and VC as a share of GDP tops the OECD ranking.

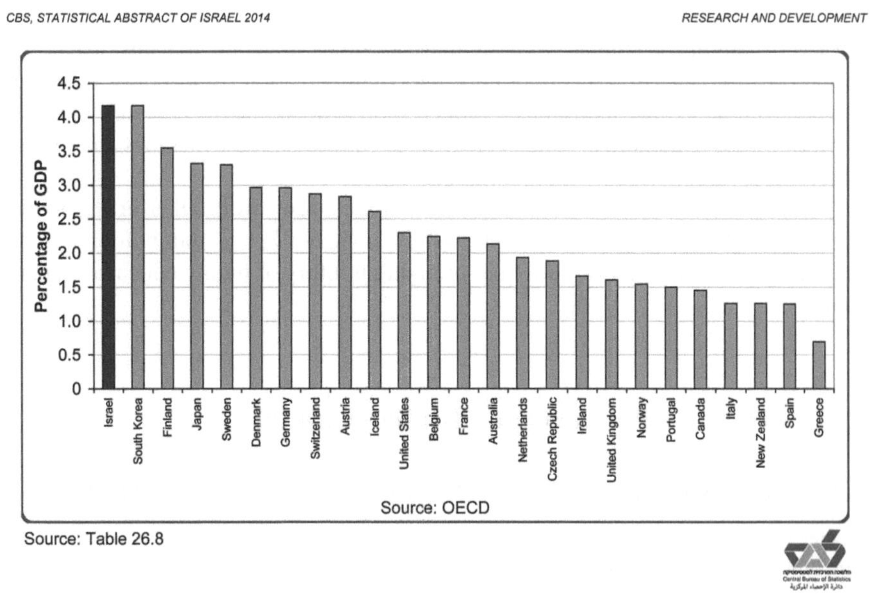

Fig. 3.2 National expenditure on civilian R&D in OECD member countries 2012

[1] It has the second highest ratio of higher education in the world.

[2] In 2000, Israel's R&D intensity was already higher than 4 % and continued to increase until 2007 when it reached 4.84 %. It then fell to 4.2 % in 2012 – a value more than double the EU average.

Half of the total R&D expenditure as a share of GDP is foreign, while the EU average is around 10 %: an indicator of the degree of internationalisation of business R&D as well as the country's attractiveness for foreign investors (Nelson 1993).

Importantly, the above figures *exclude the significant defence R&D*. We assess the share of the defence R&D as *an additional 1–1.5 % of the GDP*, thus bringing the Israeli R&D expenditure close to 6 % of the GDP.

This innovation ecosystem is the result of the grand strategic goal to strive for qualitative advantage. We now turn to present the ecosystem's cultural, structural, and organisational elements.

3.3 Culture and Human Capital

The crucial importance of cultural values in driving innovation is increasingly recognised in current research (The 3rd Annual Cyber Security International Conference 2013). The Jewish historical tradition of scholarship developing the art of interpretation to meet modern needs has found a new ground in modern Israel. In Israel, the looming security threat created a culture of improvisation and 'make-do', creatively solving problems with limited resources at hand. Broadly speaking, Israelis are characterised by direct informal communication; short power distance[3] and perception of equal status; task-oriented approach; boldness (*Hutzpah*); minimal a-priori respect to authority—often perceived as rudeness. These qualities and formal education are developed by the Israeli ecosystem.

In addition, the massive immigration of skilled Jews from all over the world enriched the human capital. A recent example is Soviet Jewry immigration[4] —one million in a decade— since 1989 that brought an influx of highly educated human capital.

3.4 Structural Elements and Human Capital

3.4.1 The Military Service and Human Resource Development

The unique role of the IDF needs further explanation. To counter the vast geopolitical inferiority in the region, and to maximise the defence forces since the 1948 War of Independence, the IDF devised compulsory conscription of 2 years for females and 3 years for males, plus subsequent reserve duty. An elaborate system developed to

[3] Power distance measures the distribution of power within a society in terms of the degree to which its members expect and accept inequality.

[4] The 82,000 Soviet-trained engineers joined the workforce of some Israeli 30,000 engineers often resulting in overqualified work placement.

maximise IDF effectiveness by improving the human capital before and during military service, driven by the strategy to strive for quality.

A screening process allows IDF human resources (HR) to assess the candidates' qualities prior to recruitment, and then continually re-assess them during their service. To serve in positions that demand extensive training, the candidate must agree to longer than mandatory periods of service. Several institutional arrangements such as The Academic Reserves (*Atuda*) enable every year about 1000 capable high school students to pursue a university diploma (particularly in science and engineering) prior to their military service.[5] On enlistment, their military service is postponed until they complete their academic studies, paid by the IDF; hence the name 'reserves'.[6] After they complete their studies, they join the IDF and usually serve as officers in a position that fits their professional knowledge gained; their 3 years compulsory service is prolonged by 3 to 5 years with full salary and benefits. As a result, scientists/engineers and programmers in the IDF will join the Israeli workforce as engineers after they finish their service, which usually lasts 6–10 years (Paikowsky and Ben Israel 2009). Israel has the highest concentration of engineers in the world—135 per 10,000 people, compared to 85 per 10,000 people in the United States which stands in the second place.

Talpiot ('magnificent building') is an elite 40-month IDF training programme for outstanding high school graduates, established in 1979, run by *Maf'at* (*Defence R&D Directorate*).[7] It is a particularly good example of a government programme having significant spillover effects on long-term innovation through human capital investment by developing entrepreneurial and applied technological skills during IDF service.

The IDF, through its many technological units, became the main stimulus for the diffusion of computer technologies and their application throughout the economy (Breznitz 2002). In addition to many in-house IT courses, since 2012 the IDF began the Cyber Shield course, training soldiers to protect the military's core systems in cyberspace.[8]

3.4.2 *Miluim (Reserve Duty)*

Reserve duty was designed to maximise fighting power. Despite the 11-fold increase in the Israeli population since 1948, reserve duty remains a prominent reality for many Israelis. Men and women serve in reserve until age 40 or 50 (depend on their

---

[5] That is close to 1 % of the cohort every year.

[6] Another program, the Technologic *Atuda* involves technician or a practical engineer diploma; in this program the training is shorter and takes place in colleges instead of universities.

[7] The members pursue a BSc in Physics and Mathematics or Computer Science at the Hebrew University in Jerusalem in Air Force uniform while undergoing periods of field training designed to familiarize them with all branches of the IDF.

[8] www.idf.il/1283-18154-en/Dover.aspx

military occupation). Among them, smaller subgroups of highly qualified personnel are retained in their units and are recalled to serve as technicians or developers. These reservists especially serve as a conduit between industry, academia, the government, and the IDF. Moreover, they provide unofficial points of contact, creating a strong multi-cohort network. The reserve service plays an important and complex role in the creation, development, and sustainability of the Israeli innovation ecosystem.

3.4.3 Organisational Culture

Due to the high intensity of the continuous engagement with immediate challenges, the organisational culture of the IDF is mission-oriented. IDF soldiers and officers in non-combat situations are expected to improvise to achieve their mission, even if this means breaking some rules. Creativity and intelligence are highly valued, no less than the authority of formal education or ranks. IDF service provides experience-exerting responsibility in a relatively non-hierarchical (for a military) environment. The service creates a mind-set where that considered risky in most Western democracies is unimpressive in comparison to the high-pressure environment, not to mention combat situations. Advanced technical skills, acquired via military training and practical experience, contribute to maturity and increased self-confidence. The social networks with peers, commanders, and reservists created during the service help make new connections and provide consultation.

Generally, the IDF serves as the first employer for the workforce during one's formative years. Military service brings with it professional training, social ties, and a work ethic that influence the hi-tech workforce and hi-tech industry's culture. An institutional preference for employees who have had meaningful service in technological or combat units is evident in the job market. The practical experience gained in advanced technologies and leadership combined with military service is valued as par with a diploma: hi-tech jobs in the Israeli media commonly require a 'degree in computer science *or* a graduate of a technological unit' (Swed and Butler 2013).

3.4.4 Defence R&D and IDF Technological Units

Israel's large and classified defence R&D carries out extensive thematic research which sometimes comes to fruition in advanced integrated IT-intensive systems, such as intelligence acquisition and processimg, precision-guieded munitions, UAVs and active missile defence. We estimate the defence R&D volume as 1.5 % of the GDP. Israel utilises the academic and industrial institutions rather than a dedicated military academy or a defence research institute.

Maf at – The Directorate of Defence R&D (DDR&D) in the Ministry of Defence (MOD) (MOD DDR&D) run jointly with the IDF, is responsible for sponsoring and enhancing advanced scientific infrastructure, facilitating the development and enhancement of defence technology for the creation of high-impact technological opportunities. It supports developing technologies, from components to full weapon systems, and combat-support equipment. The directorate commissions defence R&D, including future concepts for a competitive advantage on the battlefield even without the armed services' formal requirements. *Maf'at* is coordinating R&D projects between the IDF, research institutions, the defence industries, and relevant government arms, e.g., the Israeli Space Agency.

3.5 The Business Sector Role in Civilian R&D

The business sector accounts for around 80 % of total R&D expenditure in Israel (Fig. 3.3).

Business Expenditure on Research and Development (BERD) as a share of GDP is the second highest in the OECD (Fig. 3.4).

This high share of BERD is also explained by the grand strategy that strives for qualitative advantage to counterbalance quantitative inferiority. The Israeli economy has long emphasised R&D and innovation as essential. Research in fields such as agricultural engineering, minerals, chemistry, pharmaceutical, etc. are constant features of the Israeli economy. The capabilities developed and deployed for military and intelligence purposes both in the military and civilian sectors have produced a

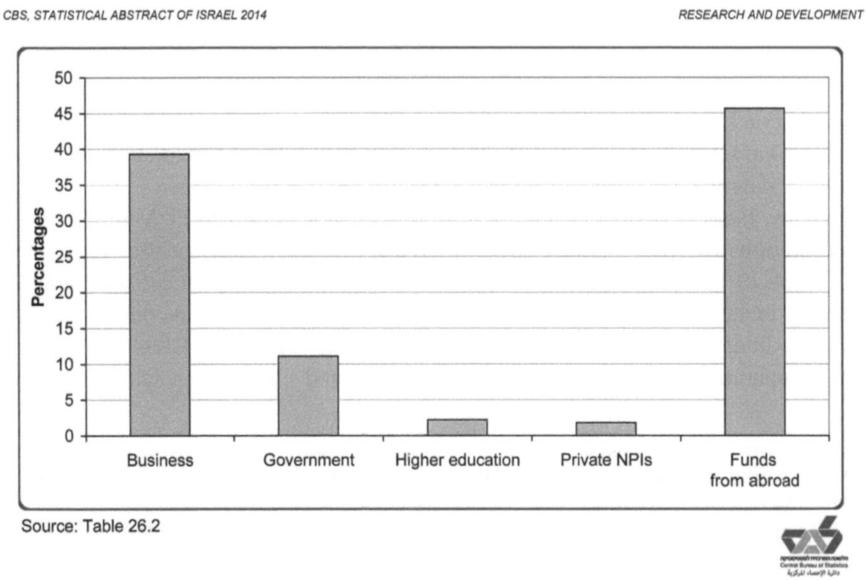

Fig. 3.3 National expenditure on civilian R&D, by financing sector 2011

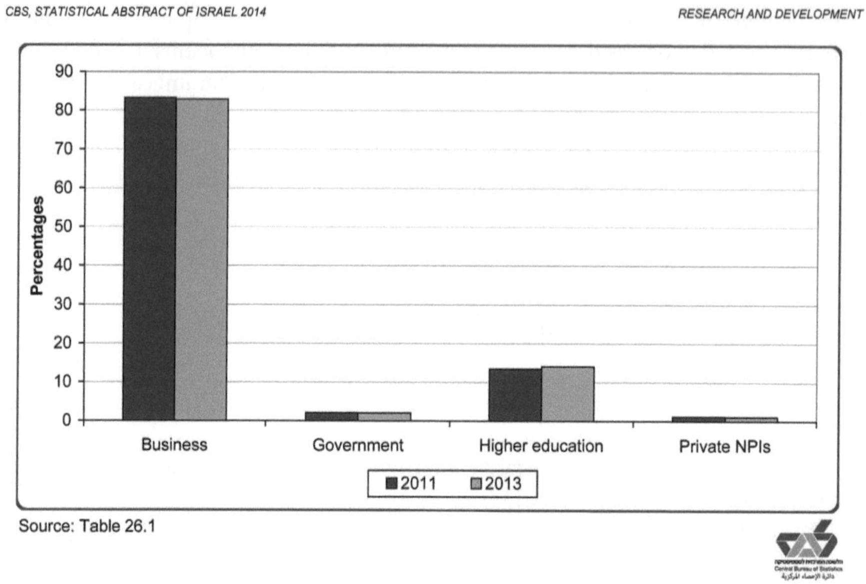

Fig. 3.4 National expenditure on civilian R&D, by operating sector 2011, 2013

significant spillover effect into the economy. Alumni of the IDF have gone on to found many Israeli IT start-ups and companies, partially due to the open innovation and knowledge transfer policy (Senor and Singer 2009). The domestic defence industry has grown dramatically since the abrupt French arms embargo in 1967,[9] and later developed into a knowledge-intensive, export-oriented high-tech sector focusing on knowledge-intensive solutions rather than major battle platforms (Efrat 2014). Due to the high costs of R&D and the small domestic market unlike other national defence industries, Israel relies heavily on export.[10]

Today, Israel hosts R&D centres from most major high-tech IT Multi National Corporations (MNCs)[11] (Haan 2011). Increasingly, these R&D centres have been the result of a multinational firm acquiring an Israeli start-up in software and IT security niches. Starting in the 1970s, large high-tech multinational companies such as IBM, Intel, and Motorola started to establish R&D centres in Israel attracted by the comparatively cheap, high-quality scientific and engineering labour and the

[9] After the Six-Day War in June 1967, Charles de Gaulle's government imposed an arms embargo on the region, mostly affecting Israel.

[10] The major defence corporations are Israel Aerospace Industries; RAFAEL; Elbit Systems and Israel Military Industries.

[11] Including Intel, IBM, Microsoft, Google, HP, Yahoo!, Facebook, Oracle, SAP, Cisco, Siemens, EMC.

various government incentives to foreign direct investment. At least one-third of Israeli export is associated with IT while only about 7 % of Israel's human capital (approximately 200,000 employees) works in the IT sector.

3.5.1 The Start-Up Scene

In 2011, 3,850 start-ups[12] were active in Israel, that is, one start-up per 2,000 citizens. According to Senor and Singer, this intensity stems from several factors: the Jewish culture of doubt and argument, where leadership can always be reasonably questioned; military service experience and (Soviet-Jewish) immigration (Senor and Singer 2009). We too have discussed these factors earlier in this section, but frame them into the larger picture of grand strategy.

The success of the VC industry in Israel started with *Yozma* ('initiative'), the 1993 government programme offering attractive tax incentives to foreign VC investments in Israel and matching their investment with government funds.[13] In the past decade, the total annual investment by VCs in Israeli technology start-ups has been four times higher than the total government budget to support innovation in all firms {García-Torres, 2014 #1755}. 'Angel' investors[14] have become more recognised as a capital source; incubators and accelerators[15] continue to attract new members.

3.6 The Government and Legal Conditions

Government policies and law play key roles in fostering (or hindering) innovation worldwide. The Law for the Encouragement of Industrial Research & Development (1984 R&D Law) purpose is to encourage Israeli companies to invest in R&D projects, with the Government sharing in the risk inherent in such projects. The main regulations under the R&D Law are Royalties and Intellectual Property. Research and innovation are initiated throughout the economy and government, and are influenced by several separate departments. Ministry of Finance has the keys to the treasury and can provide funds via the annual budget appropriations, while Ministry of Education can influence the high-school curriculum and infrastructure. However the main governmental player is the Ministry of Economy.[16]

---

[12] Most of the start-ups are in the IT sector, others are in medical devices, cleantech and green technology.

[13] In 1985, the past Chief of Staff of the Israel Air Force founded the first Israeli venture capital (VC) fund.

[14] A wealthy individual who provides capital for a business start-up.

[15] Accelerators are short-term programs in which entrepreneurs focus on training and mentorship to develop their business model.

[16] Formerly the Ministry of Industry, Trade and Labour.

3.6.1 *Ministry of Economy: The Office of the Chief Scientist*

The Office of the Chief Scientist (OCS) oversees all government sponsored support of civilian R&D in the Israeli industry. The role of the OCS is to reduce the risk of innovation in firms by shouldering part of the costs. In most cases, if the innovation project succeeds, companies repay royalties to the OCS. Otherwise, there is no need to pay the government back. However, it is important to stress that the OCS does not regard itself as an investor. Through Israel's Industry Center for R&D (*Matimop*), the executive agency of the Office of the Chief Scientist (OCS) runs 29 bilateral international agreements. The three major instruments currently in place are: the R&D Fund, which funds innovation projects in all firms; the incubator[17] framework which supports start-ups; and the *Magnet* Organisation which deals with pre-competitive R&D through collaboration between the academia and industry.

3.6.2 *Ministry of Science, Technology and Space*

The National Council for Research and Development (*Molmop*) in Ministry of Science consists of representatives of the public sector, academia and the private sector. The council serves as an advisor to the government.[18] The Israel Academy of Science develops strategic plans for the future scientific development. The *Committee of Infrastructure* advises the Ministry of Science on national science infrastructure issues.

3.7 Academia

Most of basic research and higher education are conducted by the seven public research universities (in order of age): The Technion—Israel Institute of Technology; The Hebrew University of Jerusalem (HUJI); Weizmann Institute of Science (WIS); Bar Ilan University (BIU)[19]; The University of Haifa[20]; Tel Aviv University (TAU)[21];

---

[17] Incubators are programs, lasting for 1 to 2 years, designed to help startup companies in their early stages providing office space, administrative staff, as well as mentorship and networking with experts. Israel has about 20 incubators which are private enterprises highly financed by the government.

[18] One of the authors – Isaac Ben Israel – serves as the Chairman of the Molmop.

[19] Est. in 1955 BIU aims to forge closer links between Torah and universal studies.

[20] Est. in 1963.

[21] Est. in 1968 Israel's largest and most comprehensive institution of higher education is home to over 30,000 students, half of them are graduate students, studying in nine faculties and over 125 schools and departments across the spectrum of sciences humanities and the arts. It ranks first in research output and first in citation impact among Israeli institutes. Both authors are affiliated with The Yuval Ne'eman Workshop, and the Blavatnik ICRC at TAU.

and Ben-Gurion University of the Negev (BGU).[22] Three of the seven (The Technion,[23] HUJI,[24] and WIS[25]) were established *before* the creation of the State of Israel, as its forefathers envisioned a central role for culture, education, and science for nation-building efforts.

3.7.1 Public Research Universities

Today, Israeli universities are competing globally.[26] The global recognition of its research quality is confirmed by Israel's remarkable success as an associated country in the EU's Seventh Framework Programme (FP7)[27] (Nelson 1993). The share of the GERD financed from abroad increased from 28 % to 47 % over 2007–2011;

---

[22] Established in 1969 to promote the development of the Negev desert that comprises most of Israel's land.

[23] Established in 1912, the Technion is the oldest university in Israel. It has earned a global reputation for its pioneering work in nanotechnology, life sciences, stem cells, water management, sustainable energy information, technology, biotechnology materials, engineering, aerospace, and industrial engineering. Three Technion professors have won Nobel Prizes in the past 9 years. It is one of the top 100 universities worldwide (Shanghai ranking) and one of the only 10 universities in the world to have designed, built, and launched satellites.

[24] Opened in 1925, among the HUJI founders were Albert Einstein, Martin Buber, and Chaim Weizmann. HUJI has had eight Nobel Prize winners and one Fields Medal winner in mathematics in recent years.

[25] WIS was founded originally as the Sieff Institute in 1934. The driving force behind its founding was Dr. Chaim Weizmann, a world-renowned chemist who headed the World Zionist Movement for many years and served as the first president of the State of Israel. At the University of Manchester, the Russian-born Weizmann developed a new biotechnological method to produce acetone from starch through a fermentation process. After patenting his invention in 1916, he offered it to the British Navy knowing that the navy required great quantities of acetone to produce explosives. Weizmann was appointed by Churchill to head the British Navy's laboratories and was responsible for the successful production of acetone for the British war effort during WWI. The Balfour Declaration in 1917—the world's first official diplomatic move recognising Zionism—is seen as the expression of British gratitude to the ardent Zionist. Three Nobel laureates and three Turing Award laureates have been associated with the Weizmann Institute of Science. Computer science in Israel began in 1947 at the Weizmann Institute before the creation of the state.

[26] Cooperation agreements valued at hundreds of millions of dollars have been signed between leading Israeli and Chinese universities. Recently together with Cornell University, the Technion won an international competition to establish a research institute in New York City. In May 2014, Tel Aviv University and the Tsinghua University in Beijing signed a milestone agreement to establish the XIN Centre committed to jointly investing $300 million in a joint nanotechnologies research project with medical optics water treatment and environmental applications. The Technion Guangdong Institute of Technology (TGIT) – sponsored by the Li Ka Shing Foundation with a $130 million grant – is an unprecedented cooperation between the Technion, Guangdong Province Government and Shantou Municipal Government and Shantou University to develop a leading technological school in China.

[27] Israel's 1816 participants (out of 8602) rate above the EU average, receiving more than EUR 747 million of which almost two-thirds went to universities. In 2010, FP7 funding was almost on par with Israel Science Foundation funding.

the EU's Horizon 2020 will remain of central importance to the national innovation ecosystem.

Israeli universities are ranked among the top 50 academic institutions in the world in chemistry, mathematics and natural sciences and engineering. As for cybersecurity, Israeli universities host four top-50 Computer Science departments in the Technion, Weizmann Institute, HUJI, and TAU (Kon et al. 2014).

Government investment in Israeli higher education and research dwindled during the first decade of the twenty-first century, causing brain drain that became an acute problem. A strategic decision was made in 2010 to incentivise the return of externally based Israeli researchers back into national academia and industry.[28] The government budgets authorized some $1.5 billion annually higher education institutions, and the academic freedom of the universities is structurally secured via the Council of Higher Education (CHE) and its Planning and Budgeting Committee (*Vatat*).

3.7.1.1 Technology Transfer

All universities have technology transfer companies (TTC) to provide the legal frameworks for commercialization inventions made by faculty, students, and researchers, protecting discoveries with patents and working jointly with industry leaders to bring scientific innovations from the laboratory to the market. These companies serve as a liaison to industry, bringing promising scientific discoveries made at the university to industry's attention, and provide mutually beneficial results, facilitating the commercialisation of research fruits.[29]

3.8 Cybersecurity Efforts in the Innovation Ecosystem

As part of the National Cyber Initiative (to be discussed in Chap. 6) the government attempted to shift the Hi-Tech Ecosystem towards Cyber Technology, including build-up of academic knowledge, nurturing human capital etc. Some of these steps are discussed below.

---

[28] A six-year plan (I-CORE program) to revive higher education and university-based research launched in 2011. The plan calls for a 30 % increase in budgets, a doubling of funding for competitive grants, and a 9 % increase in the number of researchers. The plan provides for the creation of 20 new I-CORE research centres.

[29] A central example is Copaxone®, the innovative multiple sclerosis drug developed in Israel, patented by the Weizmann Institute TTC in 1971, licenced to Teva Pharmaceuticals in 2007, and generating significant royalties for the institute.

3.8.1 Workforce Development

There a clear need to enlarge the pool of educated youth capable of filling the ranks of growing cyber industry. This need applies to the IDF as well. This has led the IDF to initiate and support educational initiatives in the civilian school system, most recently for cybersecurity.

The *Magshimim* ('accomplishers') extracurricular programme, a cooperation between the IDF, Ministry of Education, and NGOs, focuses on the training and development of cyber skills[30] by exceptional pupils in the geo-social periphery. The afterschool programme extends from the 10th to the 12th grade. The government, IDF, and NGOs cover the costs while parents pay a symbolic fee. The *Gvahim* ('heights') curricular programme prepares pupils for a matriculation exam in cyber-security, in addition to the highest level of math and computer science. The pilot programme plans to expand to include some fifty schools.

3.8.2 Cybersecurity Business

The same grand strategy that led to the innovation ecosystem is driving cybersecurity business. According to the Israel National Cyber Bureau (INCB), Israeli exports of the cybersecurity software and services sector are second only to the U.S. In recent years, over 200 cybersecurity start-ups operate in Israel (Cheung et al. 2014). In the past 4 years alone, over 100 new cybersecurity companies have sprouted up in Israel, with nearly USD 400 million invested in 78 companies during this period, mostly by venture capitalists.

But this is not only about the start-ups. The large industries cooperate with the early-stage entrepreneurs. In 2014, over 220 local companies alongside 20 foreign R&D centres developed security solutions, applied globally, recruiting hundreds of local employees in the process.

In February 2014, the Israel Electric Company (IEC) opened 'CyberGym': a joint venture between young entrepreneurs and the IEC, to train employees in cyber-defence, and to generate new revenue for the IEC from this line of business.

3.8.3 Tel Aviv University Cybersecurity Efforts

Tel Aviv University's Blavatnik Interdisciplinary Cyber Research Centre (ICRC) was inaugurated in September 2014 in the presence of Prime Minister Benjamin Netanyahu during the 4th Annual Cybersecurity Conference held by TAU's Yuval

[30] Taught by experts from the IDF and academia and encompasses computer languages and algorithmic thought skills; computers and network architecture; and developing analytical ability and creative thought. In addition, the program includes visits to high-tech industries Intelligence Corps bases and a summer camp.

Ne'eman Workshop. The TAU and Israel's National Cyber Bureau established the centre to facilitate research in the cyber-sphere. It is the first institutionalized Israeli government-academia cooperation in cyber-related research.

The centre builds on TAU's researcher excellence and 12 years of the active cybersecurity policy-oriented university research hub: The TAU Yuval Ne'eman Workshop (YNW).

Professor Isaac Ben-Israel,[31] in conjunction with the Harold Hartog School of Policy and Government and the Security Studies Programme, established the Yuval Ne'eman Workshop for Science, Technology, and Security in 2002 at Tel Aviv University. Cybersecurity policy became the focus of YNW research and public activities: the senior cyber-forum regularly convenes top executives with TAU researchers, government representatives, and investors. This informal platform facilitates cooperation, which helps to overcome the traditional barriers among academia, business, industry, defence, and government. Since 2011, the Annual International Cybersecurity Conference attracts thousands of visitors to the university.[32] Recognising the growing impact of cyberspace, in 2010, Prime Minister Netanyahu set up the National Cyber Initiative taskforce headed by Professor Ben-Israel. This became a major milestone in Israeli policy, discussed in the following chapter.

3.8.4 *Be'er-Sheva*

Ben-Gurion University in Be'er-Sheva, the adjacent Soroka Medical Centre, and the ongoing transfer of IDF technology units to a new desert campus are the cornerstones of the government's effort to boost economic and social development of the Negev Desert. Prime Minister Netanyahu drives the efforts to make Be'er-Sheva 'the cyber-capital'. The Israel National Cyber Bureau (INCB),[33] Ben-Gurion University and the IDF are establishing an international cyber research centre in the Advanced Technologies Park adjacent to the university's Marcus Family Campus, called 'CyberSpark'. Its first building will host Lockheed Martin, IBM, Deutsche Telekom, EMC (RSA), Jerusalem Venture Partners (JVP), Elbit and the technology transfer company of the university.

3.9 Conclusion

Cybersecurity in Israel is best understood in context of the Israeli grand strategy, in particular the role of science and technology in the search for qualitative edge to offset geopolitical inferiority, and the resulting Israeli national innovation ecosystem.

[31] Ben-Israel co-authored this SpringerBrief.

[32] http://sectech.tau.ac.il/cyberconference/

[33] See Ch. 7–8.

The unique IDF recruitment, human resource development, and reserve service shape human capital development, in addition to education, academic and business experience. The defence sector has sustained a large R&D effort for decades, creating significant spillover effects. The government creates mechanisms to incentivise R&D, including the VC scene. The public research universities conduct basic research, and participate in most of the applied research. TTCs bridge the gap between academic research and technology commercialization. Moreover, recent cybersecurity policy efforts trace back to Tel Aviv University. The business sector attracts domestic industry R&D efforts, followed by multinational companies R&D investment which benefit from the human capital, risk-taking entrepreneurial culture, and scientific infrastructure.

The Israeli national innovation ecosystem enabled current Israeli technology and human capital prowess, cybersecurity included. Fueling the ecosystem with extraordinarily high rate of R&D expenditure will help Israel adapt to the future economic and security challenges.

References

Breznitz D (2002) The military as a public space: the role of the IDF in the Israeli software innovation system, vol 13, Working papers. Samuel Neaman Institute for Advanced Studies in Science and Technology, Haifa

Cheung TM, Mahnken TG, Ross AL (2014) Frameworks for analyzing Chinese defense and military innovation. In: Cheung TM (ed) Forging China's military might: a new framework for assessing innovation. Johns Hopkins University Press, Baltimore

Efrat K (2014) The direct and indirect impact of culture on innovation. Technovation 34(1):12–20. doi:10.1016/j.technovation.2013.08.003

García-Torres A (2014) ERAWATCH country reports 2013: Israel ERAWATCH country reports (Report EUR 26765 EN ed.). European Commission Joint Research Centre Institute for Prospective Technological Studies, Luxembourg

Grissom A (2006) The future of military innovation studies. J Strateg Stud 29(5):905–934. doi:10.1080/01402390600901067

Haan UD (2011) The Israel case of science and technology based entrepreneurship: an exploration cluster. In: Mian SA (ed) Science and technology based regional entrepreneurship global experience in policy and program development. Edward Elgar Publishing, Inc., Cheltenham

Kon F, Cukier D, Melo C, Hazzan O, Yuklea H (2014) A Panorama of the Israeli software startup ecosystem. Orit and Yuklea, Harry, A Panorama of the Israeli software startup ecosystem (March 1, 2014)

Lundvall B-Å (2010) National systems of innovation toward a theory of innovation and interactive learning. From http://dx.doi.org/10.7135/UPO9781843318903

Nelson RR (1993) National innovation systems a comparative analysis. Oxford University Press, New York

Paikowsky D, Ben Israel I (2009) Science and technology for national development: the case of Israel's space program. Acta Astronaut 65(9–10):1462–1470. doi:10.1016/j.actaastro.2009.03.073

Schwab K (2013) The global competitiveness report 2013–2014. World Economic Forum, Geneva

Senor D, Singer S (2009) Start-up nation: the story of Israel's economic miracle. Twelve, New York

Swed O, Butler JS (2013) Military capital in the Israeli Hi-tech industry. Armed Forces & Society, 0095327X13499562

Taylor MZ (2012) Toward an international relations theory of national innovation rates. Secur Stud 21(1):113–152. doi:10.1080/09636412.2012.650596

The 3rd Annual Cyber Security International Conference. In: Tabansky L (ed) Tel Aviv University, The Yuval Ne'eman Workshop for Science, Technology and Security: 3rd annual Cyber Security international conference Tel Aviv, 2013: The Yuval Ne'eman Workshop for Science, Technology and Security

Chapter 4
Mid-1990s: The Prequel for National Cybersecurity Policy

Abstract This chapter describes the commencement of national cybersecurity policy in Israel, as evident in non-military information assurance efforts, early e-government and Web services, and Internet connectivity. The policy adopting was relatively slow and far from what IT-security personnel advocated; only some civilian sectors of the government reluctantly started to pay attention to information security. The erroneous expectation that computers alone would improve cybersecurity receives repeated disappointment.

Keywords Disruption • Information assurance • Critical infrastructure • e-Government • *Tehila* • Distributed denial-of-service attack (DDoS)

4.1 Bridging the Knowledge Gap Between Defence and Civilian Government

Within the Defence community, those involved with cyber technology in the relevant agencies comprehended that penetration into computer systems provides considerable advantages. We reiterate that the Israeli Defence Force and intelligence services in particular paid close attention to computing and electronics, and pushed technological developments in several directions, including aspects related to encryption and information security. Naturally, the details remain classified.

The exhilarating opportunities in computing also carried new risks. In the mid-1990s, the importance of cyberspace for the normal functioning of society became clear to some defence leaders. Their individual attempts to involve the civilian sector are the major source for the first civilian policy initiatives. But drastic changes loomed beyond the battlefield.

In the beginning of the 1990s, the internet was starting to take a central role in communications. In 1997, IBM computer Deep Blue defeated world chess champion Garry Kasparov in a powerful demonstration of artificial intelligence. The expectations for IT grew higher. The civilian sector could no longer entirely ignore the policy implications of IT technology-driven changes.

L. Tabansky, I. Ben Israel, *Cybersecurity in Israel*, SpringerBriefs in Cybersecurity, DOI 10.1007/978-3-319-18986-4_4

4.2 Civil Government Encounters Cyberspace: Information Security and e-Government Initiatives

From the mid-1990s on, personal computers (PCs) and the Internet were increasingly disrupting business, defence, and government organisations. With the affordability of cellular telephony since 1995, military units abandoned stationary telephones and Motorola radios in favour of the comfort of their personal cellular phones. Inevitably, it was used conveniently for discussing operational plans despite the IDF Information Security Separtment efforts to educate soldiers and punish the wrongdoers. Government worker connectivity to the Internet and to local area networks was in sudden demand—one that needed supplying. Common solutions varied from a segregated Internet station through to providing two separate computers to an entitled employee, and up to a shared commercial connection, putting the office's network information security at risk. Websites were becoming the new 'must haves'. Government branches hosted their new sites insecurely at amateurish private firms, and some of those sites were breached.

In April 1995, the government resolved to establish a special department for securing 'sensitive information'. Since the very first arrangement, a clear separation of authority between defence and civilian sectors was maintained: the department excluded the defences sector that traditionally had a similar function.[1] As often happens, the government did not fully implement its own resolution. The special department for securing 'sensitive information' was established only in 1999, not before the State Comptroller office audits had criticized the government for failing to implement its own decision. The unit constructed new guidelines to secure sensitive information throughout the government on seven fronts:

- Security audits for IT systems
- Human risk-factor reduction: training and screening personnel
- Access control: passwords and biometric means
- Hardware and applications inventory
- Planning for recovery
- IT-security and data access for stand-alone and air-gapped systems.
- Preparing for remote access management

The guidelines were an attempt to design acceptable information-security management standards for the entire government, utilising the best practices available in the business sector, in an era when the issue was still in its infancy.

Later, an 'advisory board for computerised systems and information security review' was established to systematically discuss the relevant key issues. The board held 30 professional thematic sessions from February 2001 to January 2005. In conjunction to the board, various IT units implemented the recommendations separately. The efforts to integrate government IT under a single body, led by the Accountant General Department of the Ministry of Finance, achieved only partial success in limited areas.

[1] The ministerial committee for coordination and administration Decision 431/TM April 9 1995.

The information security aspects of the e-Government initiatives established in 1996 illustrate early coping with the changing environment.

4.2.1 Tehila*: IT-Security and e-Government*

The 'computer unit' in the Accountant General's office in the Ministry of Finance launched in 1996 to push a new e-government project. The Ministry of Finance had interest in increasing efficiency and cost control, as well as the bureaucratic power to drive such a cross-government move. The government computer unit became most influential in the Israeli computing market as the one shaping the government spending on technology. In 1997, the *Tehila* (Government Infrastructure for the Internet Era) unit was established to provide the government branches with these primary services towards a unified secure IT infrastructure for the whole government: secure internet access to government services, from the office and later from home; secure hosting of government websites and e-government services; and secure infrastructure to support various future government projects. *Tehila* was involved in smartcard digital ID, e-forms, *Shoham* e-payment service for fees and taxes; *Merkava* unified Enterprise Resource Planning management software (ERP); the so-called biometric database for digital identity cards of citizens, Web portals, and more. Later, *Tehila* also served as an application service provider and supported the implementation of the Freedom of Information Act.

IT-security was a central aspect of *Tehila*'s work from the start, only to increase with the expansion of services and connectivity. In recent years, the number and sophistication of intrusion attempts, the frequency and volume of DDoS attacks, as well as citizens' demand for secure and privacy-preserving electronic services has grown. Since the 2009 Operation Cast Lead, the government *Tehila* infrastructure has repeatedly withstood DDoS attacks, some at a volume larger than the 2007 attack that crippled daily life in Estonia for several weeks. Sufficient preparation by *Tehila* prevented severe immediate disruption and long-term implications. However, government IT efforts in general and IT-security in particular has never achieved the desired end-state, as many government branches were often noncompliant due to the complicated legal, budgetary, and political circumstances. The government ERP, digital ID, and many other large projects suffered major setbacks, ballooning budgets, delays, and failures.

4.3 Discussion

When it comes to the early days of cybersecurity, we often forget that the reality changed very fast. A mid-range, 2015 smartphone has more processing power than what was available to NASA to bring an astronaut successfully to the moon and back.

In the mid-1990s, we used stand-alone PCs, Intel central processing unit (CPU) topped at 150 MHz, and the typical storage measured in Megabytes (MB). The connectivity taken for granted today, let alone wireless, was once a fantasy. The phrase 'surfing the Internet', was coined and popularised in 1992, but modem connections crawled along until broadband became affordable, circa 2000. By 2007, less than 8 % of the global mobile subscribers had cellular Internet access. Google Search appeared in 1998; the volume of business e-mail only surpassed that of printed mail since 1997. The mid-1990s saw cyberspace as merely a promise, and not yet the full reality.

The initial national cybersecurity policy efforts resulted from the growing recognition by several defence leaders of the potential that technological change enabled. The government agencies situation in 1995–2002 showed localized activities in related areas rather than coherent cybersecurity efforts. The many abandoned initiatives and failed projects outweigh the few successful local initiatives. The policy efforts took a long time to materialise for three reasons: the still-low penetration of ITs, the reluctance of many stakeholders to be proactive, and the competition with other pressing topics within the overburdened Israeli government system.

Despite Israel's strategic emphasis on science and technology, which led to the availability of adequate technical capabilities and rising awareness, IT efficiency and security were far from exemplary across the government at the time.

4.4 Conclusion

This chapter presented early information assurance, e-government and Web services efforts in the Israeli government, as it was facing the unfolding Information Revolution. We must remember that some two decades ago, IT was not yet as ubiquitous as it is now, and the challenges were less pressing. Defence leaders bridging the knowledge gap to civilian branches of government drove attention to IT-security risks. But the efforts to increase productivity, efficiency and security were rather uncoordinated throughout the government, as most government agencies were able to pursue their needs independent of the *Tehila* (Government Infrastructure for the Internet Era) unit professional service. This case leads to an almost trivial conclusion: Cybersecurity is not a technical matter of measuring risk, and managing it by acquiring and implementing IT-security solutions. Cybersecurity is a *policy* issue and, as such, cultural, organisational, and political processes cannot be overlooked.

Chapter 5
The Israeli National Cybersecurity Policy Focuses on Critical Infrastructure Protection (CIP)

Abstract National cybersecurity strategy and policy in Israel commenced in the early 2000s, with a centralised Critical Infrastructure Protection, one of the first policies of its kind in the world. The regulation instated in the 2002 'Resolution B/84' mandated cybersecurity directives for selected commercial and public organisations and utilities by the National Information Security Authority. The organisations supervised by the National Information Security Authority were required to finance and implement the mandatory security instructions.

We discuss the stakeholders' encounter with the inevitable cybersecurity dilemmas and describe the policy-making process for achieving acceptable trade-offs between competing values. The Tel Aviv Stock Exchange (TASE) reluctance to accept this cybersecurity regulation illustrates the recurring challenges facing cybersecurity policy. The CIP arrangement proved viable, and is still operational in 2014, but is far from being the ultimate step in cybersecurity policy.

Keywords Cybersecurity • Critical infrastructure • Critical infrastructure protection (CIP) • Regulation • B/84 • National Information Security Authority (NISA) • *Re'em* • ISA • *Shabak* • Tel Aviv Stock Exchange (TASE)

5.1 The Responsibility for Protecting Computerised Systems in the State of Israel: Special Resolution B/84

We have already outlined the Israeli defence sector's roles in the unique innovation ecosystem. Following the understanding of civilian infrastructure and cyber-vulnerabilities accumulated after years of defence experience, *Maf'at* (the Ministry of Defense Directorate for Defense Research & Development, DDR&D) has communicated cybersecurity concerns to the other government branches. The previous attempts by the civilian government to tackle the emerging risks that were described in Chap. 4 above were increasingly perceived as unsatisfactory. The government then tasked the National Security Council (NSC) to outline strategies to cope with the emerging risks. The work resulted in the December 11, 2002 Government of Israel Special Resolution B/84 on 'The responsibility for protecting computerised systems in the State of Israel'. This resolution defined the goals and the means of cybersecurity policy in Israel.

L. Tabansky, I. Ben Israel, *Cybersecurity in Israel*, SpringerBriefs in Cybersecurity, DOI 10.1007/978-3-319-18986-4_5

As any formal document, the B/84 resolution starts with defining the conceptual foundation. The Internet and the Web often conflate with cyberspace, even today. In the 2002 resolution, the computerised information systems were defined as interconnected with physical realms; what today is referred to as 'cyberspace' was not viewed as a virtual environment, or as an independent area of operation. Moreover, an 'information' system differentiates from a 'control' system, in both concept and practice. An information system 'performs automated activities of input reception, processing, storage, processing, and transmission of information'. On the other hand, a control and supervision system is a computer-integrated system that controls and supervises the frequency and regulation of measureable activities, carried out by mechanised means within the information system itself. The B/84 resolution defines the responsibility for protecting computerised systems: it is shared by the user operating critical infrastructure, as well as the state regulators—the supervisor.

A 'user' is a supervised organisation that operates infrastructure designated critical; therefore the government intervenes in some safety and security aspects, now including IT.[1] Resolution B/84 established two additional regulators: 'the top steering committee for the protection of computerised systems in the State of Israel' and 'the national unit for the protection of vital computerised systems'. The steering committee was chaired by the NSC, comprised of senior government officials, representatives from the Bank of Israel, and the defence agencies. This was a new function aimed to create continuous organisational capability to adapt to the changes driven by the use of cyberspace. The legislative process to designate an organisation as 'critical infrastructure' provides a mechanism for the 'user' to object the decision to the relevant *Knesset* (Parliament) committee.

While the steering committee has a policy perspective, the 'national unit' provides oversight and guidance in practice to the 'user' in eight missions:

1. Periodically assess the threat landscape and present the findings to the steering committee for approval.
2. Identify potentially critical computerised systems and recommend candidates for regulation to the steering committee.
3. Develop protective doctrine and methods specifically suited to the requirements of the Israeli critical infrastructure.
4. Integrate intelligence regarding information security from the relevant sources in the defence and business communities.
5. Provide continuous professional instruction tailored to each of the supervised organisations.
6. Set standards and operating procedures for minimising the risk to critical infrastructure of supervised organisations.

[1]In fact, the existing chief security officers at government ministries already had professionally authority for physical security of the designated supervised entities. For example, the Ministry of Communications has certain authority over some aspects of the telephone company, *Bezeq*, the Ministry of National Infrastructures over the water supply company, *Mekorot*, and so forth.

7. Develop special technological expertise in the field, leveraging cooperation with partners in Israel and abroad.
8. Initiate and support research efforts applicable for developing defensive capabilities, in cooperation with the defence community.

5.2 CIP Regulation as a National Cybersecurity Policy Process

To implement the new arrangement, the 'Regulation of Security in Public Bodies Law of 1998' was amended to provide the new regulators the authority to supervise public bodies. Despite the word 'public', private ownership of 'critical infrastructure' does not diminish the authorities of the law. The law defines 'activities for protecting vital computerised systems' as 'activities required to preserve those vital computerised systems, information stored in them, confidential information related to them, as well as preventing damages to those systems or the information in question'. One of the main questions debated by the NSC was who in the country could be tasked with hosting 'the national unit for the protection of vital computerised systems'? While there are no published records on the deliberation, the range of options is evident:

- A voluntary participatory approach, likened to the Private-Public Partnership (PPP) and non-government industry groups in the US
- Criminal prevention approach: delegating authority and resources to the police
- A military defence, the traditional approach to foreign threats
- A non-military defence, using existing national security organisations
- A new task-specific statutory agency for CIP

5.3 Who Should Provide Cyber-Defence?

The concept of confronting a nation-wide security risk—entirely with the free will of profit-driven market forces—was also rejected almost instantaneously. The clear conceptual difficulty in relinquishing a core duty of the state to the market was strengthened by the already evidently misaligned market incentives.

We discussed the fact that the defence sector and especially the IDF led IT-security. However, designating the responsibility for protecting vital computerised systems of publicly- and privately-owned civilian bodies to the military would create an immense ethical and legal problem in the Israeli democracy. Given the ubiquitous connectivity of cyberspace, delineation of domestic versus foreign cease to be clear and the military has no place in domestic security. So the military approach was rejected.

Israeli law permits only *Shabak* (Israel Security Agency (ISA)) and the police to intervene in civilian matters for specific security purposes under a comprehensive legal framework and strict judicial supervision. The military has no such legal authority. The police are the most under-resourced element of the Israeli security forces, as security attention traditionally attunes to continuous external threats. At the beginning of the millennium, on top of its common criminal law and order duties, the Israeli Police Department stood inundated by confronting Palestinian terrorist activity, which intensified in the 'suicide bombers intifada', targeting Israeli citizens on the streets, cafes, and buses and reaching its peak in March 2001. In fact, most of the Israeli attention was now devoted not to curbing crime but to homeland security and counter-terrorism efforts (Tabansky 2011).

5.4 The National Information Security Authority: CIP Regulation Meets Private Ownership

An establishment of a new dedicated agency for cybersecurity at large, or for CIP specifically, was discussed. The arguments against it were the time necessary for the legislative and administrative processes; the underlying liberal ideology that opposes further complicating the already cluttered Israeli regulatory environment; and the fact that a unit that attended to information security concerns in the governmental departments, Israeli embassies abroad, and state-owned companies already existed within the *Shabak's* Protective Security Division. *Re'em* (National Information Security Agency (NISA)) enjoyed the appropriate legal foundation in the 'Regulation of Security in Public Bodies Law of 1998' and the *Shabak* Statute. It had accumulated expertise and demonstrated professional competence. For the decision makers, the reduced burden of a new legislative and organisational requirement was attractive, as the ISA already operated in a stable legal framework. Broadening the authorities to include the public and private utilities was the chosen policy. Inevitably, it resulted in a substantial expansion of the workforce and the unit's budget, which are not publicly available.

The Israeli 2002 CIP approach required the supervised organisations (the 'users') to appoint and employ dedicated IT-security personnel on its behalf, responsible for implementing the instructions of *Re'em*. The requirements were identical for both privately-owned businesses and state-owned utilities. *Re'em* auditors may access any relevant information and assets of the organisation to ensure compliance or to assess new risk vectors. The supervised organisation continues to finance all operations, protection, maintenance, upgrading, backup and recovery of its critical IT systems, including the changes, enhancements and equipment mandated by *Re'em*, and to share information and activities with the regulator. Finally, the law holds sanctions against executives of the supervised organisations that neglect the mandatory requirements set by *Re'em*.

5.4.1 Conflicts and Resolutions: The Case of Cybersecurity for the Financial Sector

As happens with any serious policy change, the implementation of the CIP arrangement has not gone smoothly. The opposition to pay the costs was a constant issue and probably caused significant delays in implementing the desired equipment and methods of protection. Another, more vocal opposition, stated issues of fundamental liberties, privacy, trust, and transparency. Most conflicts had not resonated publicly. Only one episode provides the opportunity to trace the dynamics of cybersecurity policy tensions. When NISA attempted to extend its oversight over to the commercial banking sector and the financial markets, the opposition was even more vocal.

The financial sector is a key component of a modern economy, and its contribution to the Israeli GDP grows consistently. Circa 2006, the top steering committee and NISA reached the conclusion that the Tel Aviv Stock Exchange (TASE)—with operations entirely dependent on computerised systems—should be designated as 'critical infrastructure'. The legislative process provides an organisation to object the decision and state its position on the matter to the relevant *Knesset* committee. The TASE chose vehemently to resist the proposal, utilising the official channels, the public opinion arena via the media, the financial milieu, as well as backchannels to the decision makers.

Ester Levanon, TASE CEO, presented two arguments against the decision. First, the head of the TASE personally, and the organisation as a whole have sound expertise in information security. TASE is well aware of the risk, and of the crucial role of IT-security for their mission; perhaps it has better experience than other sectors of the economy. Moreover, TASE voluntarily complies with the advanced global and Israeli IT-security industry standards. Therefore, the organisation does not need a state oversight for CIP or IT-security. Personal history is a necessary fact in this case: Ester Levanon came to manage the TASE between the years 1973 and 1985 from *Shabak*, where she had established and managed the IT department.

The second argument against regulation is more substantial and perhaps universal. The TASE participates in the global financial market to benefit the Israeli economy and well-being. Any supervision of the stock exchange's computerised infrastructure by a clandestine intelligence service could tarnish the Israeli financial market reputation beyond repair. It would result in a massive withdrawal of capital from the Israeli stock market, as investors would fear prying eyes. Global capital, which has just begun to flow to Israel following the 1990s market liberalisation, would certainly depart if any ISA supervision of TASE computers were even contemplated. These divestment decisions would happen even if the concerns were entirely unsubstantiated. Not only would TASE trade volume shrink drastically, the local economy growth would come to a halt due to decreased access to public funding via the stock and bond markets. Therefore, proposed supervision is counterproductive and strategically dangerous, as it would damage the national economy in the process of attempting to increase cybersecurity.

Though a public debate seems appropriate in such civilian security matters, the debate went on mostly behind closed doors. After much deliberation, the injunction that designates the TASE as a 'critical infrastructure'—thus subject to supervision by the NISA—was approved in 2008; apparently the two parties had reached a compromise on the details of the specific arrangement. The facts show that supervision did not bring the catastrophic results that the TASE CEO had predicted, and that Ester Levanon stayed in office until 2013. *Shabak* maintained the separation between the task of *Re'em* and other *Shabak's* duties, despite the potentially tempting gains that such encroaching could achieve.

In late 2011, *Re'em* extended its oversight to eight more companies, including commercial cellular telephony and Internet service providers (ISPs). Despite the costs mandated by regulatory guidance, recent years actually demonstrate improved cooperation among the state authorities, *Re'em*, and the dozens of critical infrastructure owners and operators. This, however, does not mean that the acute ethical, budgetary, organisational, and political dilemmas arising in cybersecurity have been solved completely.

5.5 Conclusion

This chapter presented the national cybersecurity policy era beginning in Israel in 2002 with one of the first strict national CIP policies in the world.

Cybersecurity policy is driven by the interplay of technological change, and the multitude of factors shaping the reactions of various actors in the society. The balancing of costs, market efficiency, usability, security, basic freedoms and privacy rather than technology is the core cybersecurity policy. Designing cooperation between the government and privately owned corporations remains a major policy challenge to this day. Leaving cybersecurity to market forces was no longer seen as feasible by 2002. Conversely, providing cybersecurity via the military is practically impossible in democracy. We discussed and presented the Israeli policy process and its outcome: shared responsibility, with NISA (*Re'em*) having a unique role as a mandatory professional auditor under the multi-stakeholder steering committee.[2]

The private sector's reluctance towards regulation is a powerful lingering theme in the Israeli liberal export-oriented economy. Many hold to the fact that forcing companies to comply would impede their ability to innovate, and eventually would hamper economic growth. However, the opposition to Resolution B/84 on the grounds of *Shabak* potential to intercept data in bulk was the only conflict publicly known. The arrangement remained in force 12 years later.

As cyberspace continued to expand, the voices calling for a renewed adaptation to the changing environment intensified. Far from predetermined by technological change, policy reactions result from complex interplay between social, cultural, economic, and security characteristics in the political system. Similarly, the progress described in this chapter was necessarily partial.

[2] The counter-terrorism advisor in the NSC generally chaired the steering committee.

Reference

Tabansky L (2011) Critical infrastructure protection from cyber threats. Mil Strateg Aff 3(2):61–78

Chapter 6
Seeking Cyberpower: The National Cyber Initiative, 2010

Abstract As cyberspace developed, so did the challenges. The discontent with the state of cybersecurity grew stronger in Israel. We discuss the effort to develop a more appropriate national policy, looking beyond IT-security in the critical infrastructure and defence sectors. The National Cyber Initiative was an expert multi-stakeholder external review taskforce; it pursued a comprehensive approach to cybersecurity, exploring potential macro-economic and strategic benefits for Israel on the international arena. The National Cyber Initiative taskforce's report formed the foundation for Israeli cyber strategy.

Keywords Cybersecurity • Innovation • Science • R&D policy • Multi-stakeholder • Tel Aviv University • External expert review • National cyber-initiative

6.1 Non-linear Evolution

The preceding chapters presented the Israeli efforts to address cybersecurity risks. Yet as breaches, malfunctions, corporate espionage and politically motivated leaks[1] were growing in volume and impact, the criticism of the level of cybersecurity became prevalent in Israel. The assorted cyberattacks in 2007 Estonia and 2008 Georgia stressed the urgency of policy improvement.

Prime Minister Benjamin Netanyahu approached the Israeli NSC in 2010 requesting a review on cybersecurity and Israel's policy. Apparently, the NSC did not implement this task. The prime minister then approached retired Major-General Professor Isaac Ben-Israel, who at that time was the Chairperson of the National Council for Research and Development in the Ministry of Science, to take on the review.[2] He indeed accepted this request and the National Cyber Initiative was launched in 2010 with the vision

---

[1] In 2008, an Israeli soldier Anat Kamm abused her privileged access to gather and leak thousands of classified IDF documents to *Haaretz* reporter Uri Blau. Kamm's defense and the State Prosecution struck a plea agreement in which she confessed to the possession and transfer of classified documents. She received a four-and-a-half-year sentence and was released from prison after serving 2 years. Blau was later sentenced to 4 months of community service under a plea bargain in exchange for all classified documents in his possession.

[2] Isaac Ben-Israel co-authored this SpringerBrief.

L. Tabansky, I. Ben Israel, *Cybersecurity in Israel*, SpringerBriefs in Cybersecurity, DOI 10.1007/978-3-319-18986-4_6

> To preserve Israel's standing in the world as a centre for information-technology development, to provide it with superpower capabilities in cyberspace, to ensure its financial and national resilience as a democratic, knowledge-based, and open society. ("The National Cyber Initiative" – a special report for the Prime Minister 2011)

The National Cyber Initiative dealt with three key questions:

1. How to incentivise and develop cyber-technology in Israel to ensure Israel position as one of the top-five world leader by 2015?
2. Which infrastructures are required to develop cybertechnology in Israel?
3. What arrangements are required to best deal with the ventures and threats in cyberspace?

The taskforce composition reflected the initiative's vision. For 6 months, a systematic overview of the challenges and opportunities was performed by eighty experts: defence and military representatives, academic experts, research and development institutional directors, and representatives from the relevant ministries such as defense, finance, economy, and science and technology. The work was divided into seven subcommittees, and one additional classified subcommittee. Below is a brief review of the key *unclassified* findings and recommendations ("The National Cyber Initiative" – a special report for the Prime Minister 2011).

6.1.1 Reassessment of Risks

Further examination of the cyber-risks reemphasised that specific cyberattacks or cyber-malfunctions could wreak havoc. Adversaries could amplify their power either by acting via cyberspace, or by exploiting the window of opportunity during a cyber-originated crisis.

Since the 2002 B/84 Resolution, the potential impacts of cyberattacks have grown, at least as much as cyberspace itself. Israel implemented policies for the protection of the defence sector and the critical national infrastructures (as described in Chap. 5). The government and defence sectors fended for themselves. The 2002 CIP protection arrangement was in place for several years, but it covered only the designated critical infrastructures. Israeli police dealt only with strictly criminally defined cases of cybercrime. This left the vast majority of the population – small businesses, NGOs, and the general citizenry – with no point of contact for cybersecurity related issues or services in 2010. Some types of threats received no comprehensive treatment: disruption to civil services and small-medium business sector; threats to 'concealed' computers such as navigational devices or controllers in cars; and degrading societal morale and resilience by cyber means.

6.1.2 Reassessment of Goals, Means and Obstacles

The main objective proposed was to develop and deploy ground-breaking capacity to provide Israel with cyberspace advantage. Israel's main assets identified were a first-rate academic establishment, which contributes to research and innovation; a range of state and security organisations possessing IT expertise; and an extensive high-tech sector, including world-leading information security companies. However, various obstacles for productive collaboration exist, and the National Cyber Initiative taskforce proposed remedies:

(a) Incentivise the business sector and IT industry to shift focus towards innovative cyber-research and development.
(b) Motivate the academic sector to research cybertechnology and develop workforce.
(c) Devise a policy coordination function to deal with organisational obstacles, conflicts of interest, and other problems.

Following the review of national regulations and legislation and international activity, the taskforce recommended that Israeli agencies participate in the appropriate international initiatives, especially to join the Council of Europe Cybercrime (2001 Budapest Convention).

Cryptography is essential to guard state secrets and intellectual property. The assumption that Israel has leading capacities in the relevant scientific and theoretical areas was examined and reaffirmed. Yet in terms of industrial implementation, commercialisation, and deployment, the taskforce saw Israel's scientific potential as unfulfilled. Export restrictions on cryptography-related products and solutions exemplify the hurdles that make cipher development exclusively for the local market unprofitable and drive away investment. To minimise the potential conflict between secrecy and commercial interests, enhanced collaboration between the IDF and the academic community is required.

To provide research and training, a high performance computer (HPC) is a necessary tool for simulation. However, since Israel remains outside the 1968 Nuclear Non-Proliferation Treaty (NPT), Israel cannot purchase advanced supercomputers on the global market. The taskforce concluded that Israel has super-computing competence in the defence establishment, academia, and industry; Israeli technology was the base for 48 of the 100 fastest HPCs. The major recommendation was to establish a national centre for super-computing to develop a large-scale simulation facility to meet all consumer needs. The report presents alternatives and cost assessments.

6.1.3 Opportunity, Not only Risk

As the Information Revolution has profound effects on society and economy, the taskforce recommended promoting cybertechnology as a field of national importance, similar to the Ministry of Science's identification of cognitive sciences, genetic medicine, algorithms, and alternative energy. The subcommittee for examining the academic benefits key recommendation was to establish a research excellence centre on cyber-related issues in the universities, in coordination with the 2010 I-CORE: Israeli Centres for Research Excellence plan.[3]

The private business sector, financed by export, foreign investors and multinational corporations, is fundamental in developing Israeli capacities in cyberspace. The high-technology industry develops and maintains the human capital, owns indigenous capabilities, increases the return on domestic R&D investment, and even improves the international status of the state. Yet the taskforce reemphasised that security is a public good, and the market cannot fully supply it. On the other hand, the government cannot achieve the desired state of cybersecurity alone, due to the characteristics of cyberspace and the inevitable conflicts of values. Therefore, if the state has to improve cybersecurity, it must engage the market and cooperate productively with the business sector on cybertechnology.

The government plays diverse roles in the cybertechnology market: it drives the largest domestic demand and shapes the market; it is the drives innovation as it finances basic defence and academic research and development, and supports industrial R&D efforts.[4] It performs various, sometimes uncoordinated, regulatory and taxation activities that influence international trade, import, export, investment and foreign capital availability.

The government has the tools to shift the current business focus of the high-tech sector towards the emerging cybersecurity needs.

Cybertechnology can bring significant *economic benefits*. Therefore, the taskforce recommends increasing relevant defence R&D while improving the exportability of future products; increase collaboration between government regulators, the MoD, defence industrial base, and the civilian industry to enable further cooperation while reducing the classification restrictions on business development:

- Incentivise early-stage market to foster more cybersecurity innovation
- Develop standardisation of cyber-protection criteria for commercial and public organisations to better quantify risks and improve selecting optimal solutions.

6.2 The National Cyber Initiative Main Recommendations

The findings of the subcommittees and the recommendations were integrated in a final report submitted to the government ("The National Cyber Initiative" – a special report for the Prime Minister 2011). Improved cybersecurity would result

[3] I-CORE is a tool developed as part of the Higher Education Multi-Year Reform Plan (2010) to strengthen scientific research in Israel in disciplines of national importance, provide conditions for the excellent Israeli researchers return to Israel, and accumulate a critical mass and relative advantages in select fields.

[4] See Chap. 3.

in dual – security and economic – benefits. The overall policy recommendations for national cybersecurity were clustered:

Education. Raise awareness and education throughout society, beginning with elementary schools.

R&D. Encourage the academic sector to launch multidisciplinary programs on cybersecurity. Develop knowledge, focusing on secure code development. Establish an accessible national cyber-simulator available as an infrastructure for all interested Israeli stakeholders.

Security. Develop national operational capabilities in cyberspace for routine and emergency acts while coping with moral, legal, privacy and financial challenges. Develop a state-wide protective shield based on unique Israeli technologies, developed cooperatively by scientific and industrial sectors, with the government encouraging local procurement to alleviate high development costs. Upgrade security by combining technical and legislative measures.

Opportunities. Cybertechnology offers economic, academic and international relations opportunities. These realms are often viewed as secondary to the quintessential national security perspective. However, taking these opportunities will foster innovation, improve education, develop workforce and domestic capacity, improve international relations and so forth.

The main practical recommendation was to establish a new governmental cybersecurity organisation to coordinate the policy effort – we discuss this in detail in the next chapter.

6.3 Conclusion

Following the reassessment of risks, existing cybersecurity efforts and the CIP arrangement were considered inadequate to meet with the rapidly changing environment. Alternative and additional ways to reduce the risks and increase resilience were discussed and prioritised.

The National Cyber Initiative pursued a comprehensive approach, moving beyond IT-security concerns in defense and critical infrastructure sectors towards exploring strategic opportunities for Israel on the international arena.

For the first time, the opportunities were systematically illuminated as well, leading to required policy changes. One of the likely contributing factors is the organisational one: the review was purposely external, unconfined to the bureaucratic division of government branches. The participating experts represented all the major stakeholders: government, public, industry, academia, investors, defence and intelligence services.

The National Cyber Initiative viewed the increased collaboration of government, defence, academia, and industry in the Israeli ecosystem as the best strategy to enhance national cybersecurity. The next challenge would be to implement the vision and recommendations.

Reference

"The National Cyber Initiative" – a special report for the Prime Minister (2011) Ministry of Science and Technology, National Council on Research and Development, Jerusalem

Chapter 7
The National Cyber-Strategy of Israel and the INCB

Abstract The current National cyber-strategy of Israel stemmed from the National Cyber Initiative and was declared in the Government Resolution 3611 'Advancing the national capacity in cyberspace'. The Israeli strategy aims at cyber-power, including more comprehensive defence, advanced research and development, developing cyber-technology as an economic growth engine, and leveraging cybersecurity for enhanced international cooperation. The Israel National Cyber Bureau (INCB) was established to develop and implement the strategy. The history of the INCB demonstrates the dynamics of cybersecurity policy. Among the INCB successes are developing and managing the incentives towards marked increase of cybersecurity education and research and development activities in academia, school system and industry, including the start-up scene.

Keywords INCB • National cyber-strategy • National cyber-policy • Resolution 3611 • Global cyber-power • Critical infrastructure protection • CIP • CERT • Innovation • Cyber-industry • Growth engine • Interdisciplinary Cyber Research Centre (ICRC) • Science policy

7.1 National Cyber-Strategy of Israel, 2011

The political fate of the National Cyber Initiative report discussed in Chap. 6 turned out to be unlike many other expert reviews in Israel, as the August 7, 2011 Government Resolution 3611 'Advancing the national capacity in cyberspace' adopts the taskforce's recommendations:

> To work towards advancing national capabilities in cyberspace and improving management of current and future challenges in cyberspace. To improve the defence of national infrastructures essential for maintaining a stable and productive life in the State of Israel, and to strengthen those infrastructures, as much as possible, against cyberattack by advancing Israel's status as a centre for the development of information technologies while encouraging cooperation among academia, industry, and the private sector, government ministries and special bodies. (Government of Israel 2011)

L. Tabansky, I. Ben Israel, *Cybersecurity in Israel*, SpringerBriefs in Cybersecurity, DOI 10.1007/978-3-319-18986-4_7

The strategy aims to maintain Israel's status as a top-five global cyber-power. The definitions section clarifies the strategy's scope:

- Cyberspace: the physical and non-physical domain that is created or composed of part or all of the following components: automated and computerised systems, computer and communications networks, software, computerised information, content conveyed by computer, traffic and supervisory data and the users of such data.
- Cybersecurity: policies, security arrangements, actions, guidelines, risk management protocols and technological tools designated to protect cyberspace and allow action to be taken therein.
- Civilian Space: cyberspace that includes all the governmental and private bodies in the State of Israel, excluding 'special bodies'—the Israel Defence Forces, the Israeli Police, *Shabak* (the Israel Security Agency), *Mossad* (the Institute for Intelligence and Special Operations), and *Malmab* (the MoD Directorate of Security of the Defence Establishment) responsible for defence industrial base.

7.2 INCB: A New Organisation to Promote the New Strategy

The key operational aspect was to establish the INCB in the Prime Minister's office, to promote national capability in cyberspace and to improve Israel's preparedness in dealing with the current and future challenges in cyberspace. It is charged with improving cybersecurity while advancing Israel's position as a centre of cybertechnology development by encouraging cooperation between academia, industry and the private sector, government offices, and the defence community.

The cyber-bureau's missions and tasks receive clear delineation in the Government Resolution 3611 of August 7, 2011:

> The Bureau functions as an advising body for the prime minister, the government and its committees, which recommends national policy in the cyber-field and promotes its implementation, in accordance with all law and Government Resolutions. (Government of Israel 2011)

7.2.1 Regarding Consolidation of National Cyber-Policy

Active advisory steps for the prime minister, the government, and its committees regarding cyberspace: (Government of Israel 2011)

1. To consolidate the government's administrative work and that of its committees in the cyber-field; to prepare them for their discussions, and to follow-up on implementing their decisions
2. To make recommendations to the prime minister and government regarding national cyber-policy; to guide the relevant bodies regarding the policies decided on by the government and/or the prime minister; to implement the policies and follow-up on their implementation

3. To inform all the relevant bodies, as needed, on the complementary cyber-related policy guidelines resulting from government resolutions and committee decisions
4. To advance coordinating and cooperating efforts among governmental bodies, defence community, academia, industrial bodies, businesses, and other bodies relevant to the cyber-field
5. To advance legislation and regulation in the cyber-field

7.2.2 *Regarding the Enhancement of Cybersecurity*

6. To serve as a regulating body in cybersecurity related fields
7. To determine and annually reaffirm the national threat reference in defending cyberspace
8. To formulate a national concept to deal with cyberspace emergencies
9. To conduct national and international exercises to improve the State of Israel's preparedness in the cyberspace
10. To assemble analysed information from all parties in the intelligence community regarding cybersecurity
11. To integrate the national situation status regarding cybersecurity from all relevant parties
12. To advance and increase public awareness to threats in cyberspace and mechanisms to cope with them
13. To formulate and publish warnings and information for the public regarding cyberspace threats, as well as practices for preventative behaviour.

7.2.3 *Regarding the Strengthening of Israel's Lead in the Cyber-Field*

14. To promote research and development in the cyber-field and supercomputing in the professional bodies
15. To advance the formulation of national education plans and wise use of cyberspace
16. To work to encourage the cyber-industry in Israel
17. To promote cooperation with relevant bodies abroad

7.2.4 *Assessing the INCB Initiatives*

Words of caution are required as we present and discuss some of the INCB actions during its 3-year existence: the available evidence is young and partial. To perform the missions, the INCB was allotted a NIS 2.5 billion budget for the next 5 years—about NIS 500 ($130) million a year. Therefore, the INCB is not only an advisory staff function but also a significant policy actor. Having both ‘carrots’ and ‘sticks’, the INCB can promote legislation, regulations, as well as inter-agency cooperation. The INCB has succeeded in promoting significant academic research efforts, as well as planning professional education, promoting export-oriented cyber-industry, and cementing several bi-lateral international cooperation agreements.

7.2.4.1 Public Cyber-Strategy Design

The INCB’s main task is drafting a comprehensive national cyber-strategy. Some clues of this strategy were hinted by the INCB head, Dr. Evyatar Matania, specifically mentioning the transition from ‘defence’ to ‘security’ in his keynote address to the Yuval Ne’eman Workshop for Science, Technology, and Security 3rd International Cyber Conference {, 2013 #1797}. It may indicate the intention to move towards a more proactive resilience posture. It is likely that the defence focus on the critical infrastructure is no longer viewed as sufficient, in line with the shifting national security perspective that broadens to consider individual well-being. The INCB held lengthy consultations with all the relevant stakeholders. However, the bureau has been unable to promote changes in CIP: the negotiations towards a new feasible CIP arrangement have culminated in a cardinal disagreement with other stakeholders, albeit for substantial rather than capricious reasons. During 2014, external review efforts were again commissioned, the highest government level was required to step in and the outcome will be presented in Chap. 8.

7.2.4.2 Supporting Innovation in Academia

Four research areas received national priority field status from the Ministry of Science and Technology in 2012: brain science, supercomputing and cybersecurity, oceanography, and alternative transportation fuels.

The supercomputing and cybersecurity priority field was placed under the responsibility of the INCB, in cooperation with the Ministry of Science and Technology. Investment in this field will focus particularly on topics in artificial intelligence, advanced computing, and cloud computing.

To improve the academic infrastructure in Israel in cooperation with the Ministry of Science, INCB established and competitively allocated NIS 50 million to over 20 large academic research projects in 2012 and 2013. In parallel, several dozens of new graduate research grants were competitively awarded to Israeli universities’ students by the INCB.

In 2014, the INCB reached agreements to establish dedicated research centres in two of the seven Israeli research universities. The INCB committed multi-year financial support to the centre for applied cyber-research at Ben-Gurion University, and to the ICRC established at TAU on April 2014.[1] This mechanism may extend to other Israeli universities.

[1] The authors are affiliated with TAU’s Blavatnik ICRC.

7.2.4.3 Supporting Innovation in Industry

Rami Efrati, former head of the civilian division of the Israel National Cyber Bureau, estimated that in less than 2 years [of INCB existence], the number of Israeli companies associated with cybersecurity increased from 50 to 220, raising more than USD 400 million in 78 funding cycles.

Alongside local companies, some 20 foreign-funded R&D centres in Israel developed global security solutions.[2] Multi-national corporations had established major cyber-centres in Israel, recruiting thousands of local employees in the process. As part of the vision that industry is a key economic growth engine, the INCB together with Ministries of Foreign Affairs and Economy organised the *Cybertech* 2014 Conference and Exhibition. It showcased Israeli cybersecurity start-ups, as well as established local and international companies. It was the largest exhibition of the cyber-technologies outside the US, attracting over 8,000 participants from 50 nations. Keynote speakers included the CEOs, executive directors, VPs from the biggest corporations, and government officials, including Prime Minister Netanyahu.

In October 2012, *Maf'at* (INCB and the MoD DR&D) launched a dual-use, *MASAD* (civilian and defence cyber R&D plan) to promote R&D projects that serve both civilian and defence goals on the national level.

The Office of the Chief Scientist (OCS) at the Ministry of Economy supports competitive R&D. In 2011, the OCS allocated NIS 62 million for 21 early-stage cybersecurity initiatives. In 2012, the OCS allocated NIS 90 million for 45 early-stage cybersecurity initiatives. In addition, the OCS will operate a new plan, *Kidma*, to support initiatives at the earliest (pre-seed) stage.

The INCB estimates that Israeli exports amount to some 8–10 % of the global cybersecurity market valued at USD 60 billion in 2013 by Gartner. Moreover, the INCB estimates cybersecurity R&D investment in Israel is to be 13 % of the global expenditure.

7.2.4.4 Critical Infrastructure Protection (CIP)

The INCB's vision includes a national cybersecurity centre, to achieve situational awareness, enhanced threat understanding, actionable intelligence, rapid decision-making, defensive agility, and coordinate timely incident response, assisting all stakeholders. A new Israel National Cyber Event Readiness Team (CERT-IL) is constructed in Be'er Sheva, and expects to reach full operational capacity in 2015. Its information-sharing mechanisms are yet unclear. The Government resolution 3611 outs the head of INCB as the head of top steering committee to protect computerised systems in the State of Israel, which was set up in 2002 in accordance with Resolution B/84. However, the INCB was tasked with developing an updated CIP arrangement in consultation with all stakeholders, to be presented to the government.

[2] Including PayPal, EMC-RSA, VMWare, Microsoft, Intel, Deutsche Telekom, Lockheed Martin, CA Technologies, McAfee, IBM, Cisco, and General Electric.

The decision on practical cybersecurity arrangement was postponed de-facto, until the new INCB concluded negotiations with the existing stakeholders. We discuss the legal and practical development of CIP further in Chap. 8.

7.3 Conclusion

The Government resolution 3611, adopting the National Cyber Initiative report, outlines the cyber-strategy of Israel. The goal is to maintain the Israeli status as a global cyber-power by enhancing cooperation in different sectors of society to improve cybersecurity while also achieving economic, technological, and diplomatic benefits.

Three years later, the strategic commitment remains strong. PM Netanyahu addressed the 4th International Cybersecurity Conference held jointly by the Yuval Ne'eman Workshop for Science, Technology, and Security, the Israel National Cyber Bureau, and TAU's Interdisciplinary Cyber Research Centre (ICRC) in September 2014:

> So let me reiterate: We are bolstering our defences and we are committed to maintaining Israel's position as a global cyber-power, and as such, we have to implement a policy, which protects cyberspace as an open space and as the basis for global growth. I want to assure you that Israel will always know how to use its unique strengths and knowledge to protect our country and as far as we can to protect the world's commitment to cyber growth. (2014)

The main operational decision was to establish the INCB as a coordinating body in the prime minister's office. It has the legal and financial capacity to promote policy to achieve long-term goals. The INCB has been able to establish itself and influence policy in various realms. Whether the INCB's coordination of activities in defence, academia, and industry sectors contributes optimally to the strategic goal of making Israel a top-five global cyber-power remains to be seen in the near future.

References

Government of Israel (2011) Government decision 3611: promoting national capacity in cyber space. PMO Secretariat, Jerusalem

MFA (2014) PM Netanyahu addresses the 4th international cybersecurity conference. Jerusalem, Israel

Chapter 8
Towards Comprehensive National Cybersecurity

Abstract This chapter presents the latest steps in Israeli cybersecurity policy evolution. Driven by the 2011 strategy, the government resolved to establish a National Cyber Security Authority (NCSA) in February 2015 to lead more comprehensive cybersecurity while minimising the tension between security needs and Israel's basic freedoms. In addition, paths were outlined for the government to lead cybersecurity practices by example, and to streamline standardisation of the cybersecurity services market. The background and the policy design process, leading the Israeli cybersecurity posture change, re-emphasise the crucial role of cybersecurity's non-technical aspects.

Keywords ISA • INCB • National Cyber Security Authority • NCSA • CIP • Resolution 3611 • Resolution 2443 • Resolution 2444

8.1 The Information Sharing Challenge to Cyber Situational Awareness

The 2010 National Cyber Initiative and the 2011 National Cyber-Strategy (discussed in Chaps. 6 and 7) identified a growing gap: though cyberspace is increasingly complex and interconnected, the defence confines to specific sectors and branches, e.g., government networks or critical infrastructures. Further, this leads to national situational awareness being almost non-existent. Access to information and traffic in non-government networks is necessary for national cybersecurity. The importance of multi-directional information sharing is intuitive: relevant, timely, and accurate information should help defenders leverage experience to reduce vulnerabilities and mitigate threats. From the technical point of view, situational awareness could be achieved by implementing sensors and reporting capabilities throughout the computer endpoints and networks of various organisations, then fusing big data to produce timely actionable intelligence, and finally acting upon it.

The reasons as to why such a solution did not happen are not unique to Israel: they stem from the inherent conflict of values in a democracy. Given the challenges of preserving privacy and intellectual property rights, establishing trust, producing, processing, and consuming classified information and legal restrictions, a common

L. Tabansky, I. Ben Israel, *Cybersecurity in Israel*, SpringerBriefs in Cybersecurity, DOI 10.1007/978-3-319-18986-4_8

approach to situational awareness is to promote voluntary information sharing. This has been the focus of American cybersecurity policy since its early days.[1] But the voluntary approach has yet to achieve the desired results. James A. Lewis of the Center for Strategic and International Studies (CSIS) says that voluntary information sharing is a failed remedy that should be set aside in favour of new concepts and strategies (Presidency 2011). Therefore, there is no escaping some other-than-voluntary measures for national cyber-situational awareness – which inevitably heightens the tension between basic freedoms and security needs in an open society.

8.2 The Dispute on Appropriate National Cybersecurity Organisation

Since 2002 Resolution B/84, The NISA unit in *Shabak* (ISA) has had Critical Infrastructure Protection (CIP) authority since 2002, as described in Chap. 5 above. Israeli cybersecurity policy saw voluntary measures as auxiliary, at best. The CIP policy included mandatory information sharing from its operators to NISA and then from NISA to other entities to improve their defences. However, as national, rather than sectorial, cybersecurity clearly requires more information, a broader range of policy instruments finely tuned to approach various 'customers' and the feasibility to upscale this arrangement to a nationwide level incurred controversy.

Shabak had long remarked that given the professional success of the 2002 CIP arrangement, the optimal response to the changing environment would be an expansion of NISA authority. The consensus was that mere protection is insufficient and a more proactive stance is needed. *Shabak* suggests preventive efforts via a concentration-centralized control of the necessary intelligence and operations that complement defensive measures with in-depth threat intelligence and active prevention. The concept *Shabak* promoted is similar to the Israeli counter-terrorism approach, which had learned in the most painful way that holding the last line of defence is bound to fail. Since 2000, the counter-terrorism strategy gradually turned from increasing protection at homeland to producing more intelligence and targeting individuals who were planning and carrying out terrorist violence.[2] Indeed, such an approach succeeded to subdue the Palestinian suicide terrorism by 2005: the IDF and *Shabak* were able to adapt to operational challenges and gained capabilities to

[1] It is a key element in all U.S. policy documents. Today 17 Information Sharing and Analysis Centers (ISACs), industry coalitions, education awareness, and other Public-Private Partnerships (PPPs) mechanisms are addressing the information sharing challenges in the U.S., in addition to various regulators, state and federal agencies.

[2] It is rendered legal as a doctrine of anticipatory self-defense.

identify the key hubs and nodes in the terrorist organisations' operation from Palestinian-controlled territory. Then, precision-targeted preventive strikes disrupted the terrorist organisations, while avoiding ground manoeuvre and its unacceptable collateral damage. This innovative operational capacity, previously impossible, depended technically on leveraging ITs to acquire continuous real-time intelligence from various sensors, process and distribute it via the operational network in near real-time (Tabansky 2007, 622).

Notwithstanding the operational promise of modelling national cybersecurity after counterterrorism, such cybersecurity policy would require a dramatic increase in the mandatory intelligence *Shabak* needed to collect throughout civilian cyberspace to carry out its operations. The clash of security and privacy values we discussed earlier in the book reignites. The INCB has thus pushed forward the establishment of a civilian agency to address civilian sector cybersecurity as part of its mandate to develop strategy and policy. The central argument was that removing the clandestine intelligence agency from the civilian cybersecurity front in favour of a civilian organisation would mitigate the conflict of values.

8.3 External Review

The attempts to settle the issues among the stakeholders and specifically the ISA and INCB were long overdue. In September 2014, *Haaretz* daily newspaper published that staff work on cybersecurity strategy and authority had deteriorated into a turf battle (Ravid 2014, 1654). The feasibility of a productive inter-agency working towards a new arrangement of cybersecurity for the civilian sector as the central part of the strategy had dwindled.

Resolving the dispute on appropriate national cybersecurity organisation eventually necessitated direct involvement by the national leadership. As the designated agencies were gridlocked, and the opinions throughout the stakeholders varied, a new round of governmental and external expert reviews was required to present the government with a feasible solution to the cybersecurity arrangement. Having steered the 2010 National Cyber Initiative, Professor Isaac Ben-Israel again was tasked by Prime Minister Netanyahu with producing a roadmap towards solving the cybersecurity policy gridlock. His taskforce consisted of representatives from the ISA, INCB, IDF Intelligence Corps SigInt unit, Mossad, National Security Council, Israeli Law, Information and Technology Authority (ILITA) in the Ministry of Justice, the Ministry of Strategic Affairs and other stakeholders. In addition, personal meetings were held with the Ministers of Finance, Defence, and Strategic Affairs as well as acting heads of security services and IDF branches. The recommendations Professor Isaac Ben-Israel prepared for the PM formed the basis of current policy changes.

8.4 The National Cyber Security Authority

To achieve the strategic goal of cybersecurity, a feasible solution to the conflicting values was required. At the 21/09/2014 Cabinet meeting, Prime Minister Netanyahu said:

> I decided last week to develop a national authority on the cyber issue to arrange and see to defending the entire State of Israel on the cyber issue. That is, defending not only important facilities and security agencies, but also how to defend Israeli citizens against these attacks. This is the establishment of a new authority. It is, in effect, the creation of an 'air force' against new threats and not to rely on this being carried out by existing agencies. We are in a new world; we are preparing with new forces. This has major significance for the defence of the State of Israel in the future (Prime Minister's Office, I. (2014)).

The PM named Israel National Cyber Bureau (INCB) head Dr. Eviatar Matania to lead its construction. Accepting the recommendation of the 2014 taskforce led by Professor Isaac Ben-Israel, the government decided to establish a new authority to enhance cybersecurity in the civilian sector in February 15 2015, Government Resolution 2443 (Prime Minister's Office, I. (2015).[3] This new National Cyber Security Authority (*Rashut Le'umit le-Haganat ha-Cyber*) will have received the necessary legal authority to defend the civilian sphere from cyber-threats as it constitutes an operative agency to act alongside the INCB, which continues to build and maintain the State of Israel's national strength as an international leader in the field.

The NCSA must better integrate the capabilities of the intelligence community with public open sources into the national effort, while maintaining their operational security and providing them appropriate legal authority. Legislation is required to monitor sections of civilian cyberspace for security while keeping the basic freedoms, civil rights and privacy. To mitigate the concerns, existing regulators will participate in the effort to update the legal framework of cybersecurity. The Israeli Law, Information and Technology Authority (ILITA), the personal data protection unit established in the Ministry of Justice in 2006, is one of the key stakeholders in cybersecurity policy.[4]

The NCSA consists of mostly new elements. The public Israel National Cyber Event Readiness Team (CERT-IL)[5] is Israel's national focal point for cyber security incident management and handling in order to enhance the national resilience against cyber threats. It provides a single point of contact in Israel regarding cyber security threats and incidents for international corporations, cyber security companies and other CERTs.

---

[3] Co-author, Isaac Ben-Israel.

[4] ILITA consists of three regulators: the database register, responsible for oversight and enforcement of data protection guidelines; the electronic signature register, and credit score service providers register.

[5] https://cert.gov.il/

In addition, as the subsequent February 15 2015 Government Resolution 2444 outlines, concentrated regulation, standardisation, licensing, auditing, training, instruction, public relations, and international cooperation efforts will be developed.

The new authority can streamline the complicated cybersecurity organisation, reducing the tensions stemming from existing classification, secrecy and operational security requirements. The NCSA architecture should better integrate the situational awareness needs while minimising the tensions with basic freedoms concerns such as privacy, to enhance national cybersecurity efforts (Fig. 8.1).

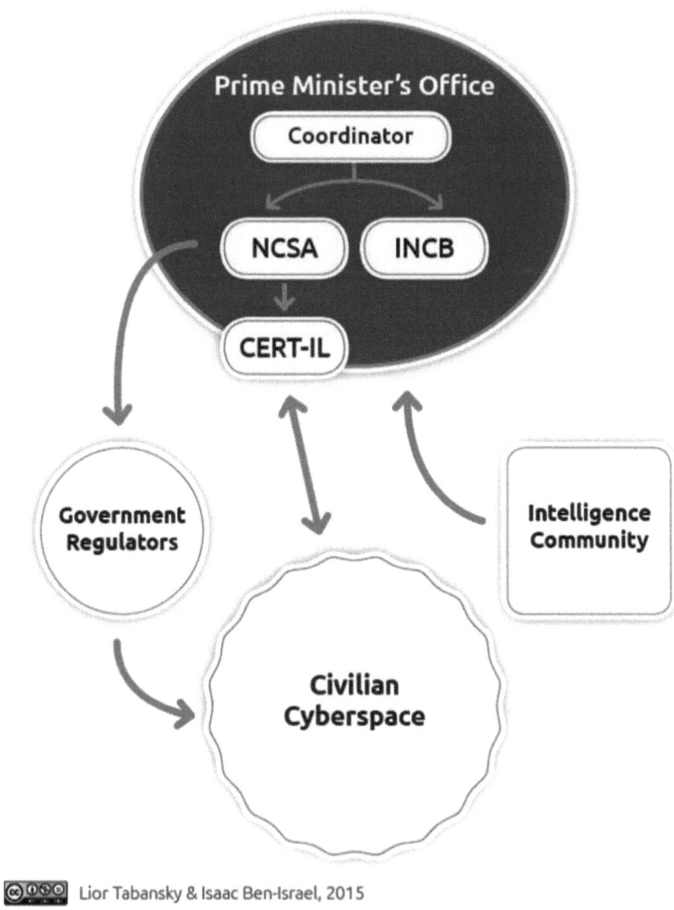

Fig. 8.1 Israel: national cybersecurity arrangement, 2015

8.5 Discussion: Generalising Policy Implications

The latest development in Israeli cybersecurity policy exemplifies that shared awareness, shared national strategy, common good will, budget, and the availability of technical capabilities are *insufficient*. The *Shabak*-INCB dispute illustrates the paradoxical importance of the non-technical aspects in technical-originated cybersecurity. The best technical IT-security or the best defence-intelligence counter-terrorism practices are inadequate for the national level. Both come in conflict with the core values of an Open Society, and the tensions must be balanced. Those concerned with cybersecurity worldwide will benefit from comprehending the societal challenges the common operational and technical security measures bring about. Effective cybersecurity policy crucially depends on the capacity to mitigate the tensions between competing values in a timely manner. Thus cybersecurity presents a severe political challenge, and requires a political solution. The organisational and personal aspects are a well-acknowledged phenomenon in business administration and public policy; these cannot be dismissed as irrational or secondary. Cybersecurity policy is not only a technical challenge but also a complex social and political task; bureaucratic politics, personal leadership, culture and other less-tangible elements are here to stay.

8.6 Conclusion

The protection of the civilian sector at large is the focus of Israeli cybersecurity policy in recent years. It presents enormous conceptual, political, ethical, legal, and financial challenges. This chapter presented the Israeli policy-making process, culminating in 2015 in the new comprehensive national cybersecurity arrangement. In 2014, Israeli leadership has overcome a hurdle, common to all the Open Societies in the Information Age: the tensions and conflict between changing security needs and the core values of a modern democracy. The NCSA design enhances comprehensive national cybersecurity while reducing the tension between security needs and basic freedoms. The process of setting up the NCSA includes multiple legislative, organisational, and other efforts aimed to last several years. Nationwide cybersecurity and cyber power depend on the political processes to mitigate complex moral and organisational tensions, rather than exclusively on scientific, technical and economic prowess to enhance IT-systems resilience.

References

Presidency, Commission on Cybersecurity for the 44th (2011) Cybersecurity two years later: a report of the Csis Commission on Cybersecurity for the 44th Presidency. Center for Strategic and International Studies. http://csis.org/files/publication/110128_Lewis_CybersecurityTwoYearsLater_Web.pdf

Prime Minister's Office I (2014) Decision to establish a new national authority for operative cyber defense http://www.pmo.gov.il/English/MediaCenter/Spokesman/Pages/spokecyber2210914.aspx

Prime Minister's Office I (2015) Cabinet approves establishment of national cyber authority http://www.pmo.gov.il/English/MediaCenter/Spokesman/Pages/spokeCyber150215.aspx

Ravid B (2014) Israeli security agencies in Turf Battle over Cyber War; Netanyahu to Decide. HaAretz, 14 Sept 2014

Tabansky L (2007) The anti-terrorism struggle in the information age: Palestinian suicide Bombers and the implementation of High Technologies in Israel's response, 2000–2005. TAU

Chapter 9
Striking with Bits? The IDF and Cyber-Warfare

Abstract This chapter presents the developments of cybersecurity and cyber-warfare in the IDF.

Cyber-warfare may be strategically advantageous if it proves less deadly and less destructive than kinetic alternatives. Logically, cyber-warfare suits the Israeli grand strategy well: either as a force multiplier or as a precision strike, it continues the quality-over-quantity principle. We utilise foreign, unconfirmed claims to discuss Operation Orchard and Stuxnet, focusing on damage assessment, effectiveness, attribution, and deterrence. Reliance on cyberattacks in high-risk operations with strategic consequences attests to the maturity of cyber-warfare capabilities. However, military capacity is just one element of national cybersecurity.

Keywords IDF • Cyber-warfare • C4I • IAF • Unit 8200 • Institute for National Security Studies (INSS) • Operation Orchard • Natanz • Stuxnet • Olympic games • Attribution • Deterrence

9.1 The IDF Perspectives on Cyber-Warfare

In Chap. 3, we discussed the quintessential role the IDF plays in human capital development, innovation, R&D, and operational experience for the Israeli technology sector. This chapter deduces its view from the scarce, mostly foreign public sources to illuminate cyber-warfare aspects in the IDF. Cyber-warfare and public references attributable to cyber-warfare have been almost non-existent, largely because of classification. Penned by an unidentified senior officer, the IDF journal *Maarachot* featured one of the first articles on cyber-warfare in 2000 (Ben-Israel 2011 #807;18# 2000, לארשי־ןב).

The Israeli Air Force (IAF), C4I Corp, and Intelligence Corps have long embraced the technological and operational aspects of the computer revolution to perform their missions, especially advancing cypher, electronic warfare, signal intelligence and computer security. Brigadier General (Ret.) Pinchas Buchris, the then Director General of the Israeli Ministry of Defence says in a 2007 interview:

L. Tabansky, I. Ben Israel, *Cybersecurity in Israel*, SpringerBriefs in Cybersecurity, DOI 10.1007/978-3-319-18986-4_9

> I can only say we're following the network attack technology with great care. I doubted this technology five years ago. But we did it. Now everything has changed. Any such capabilities are top secret. (Fulghum et al. 2007)

The IDF has recently eased the limitations on high-ranking officers to discuss its efforts. Major General Amos Yadlin, a fighter pilot who then was the Director of Military Intelligence, caused a media stir when in a 2009 public lecture he stated that *cyber-warfare suits Israel well,* and the young soldiers he meets in Military Intelligence are a source of inspiration for Israeli cyber-warfare capability (Baram 2013). Maj. Gen. Yadlin's comments during this rare public appearance were the first public acknowledgement of just how serious the Israeli military views the use of cyberspace:

> Cyber is as important to warfare today as the advent of air support was to warfare in the 20th century. It combines all the elements of a military dimension: intelligence gathering, defence and offence [...] Cyberspace can grant the small and weak the ability once held only by superpowers. [...] Like unmanned aircraft, [cyber-forces] can strike... without risking service [members'] lives. Everything is made locally without the need for foreign aid, in an area with which young Israelis are highly familiar. (Ben-David 2010)

The forum for the comment was a conference at the Israeli INSS, a reputable think-tank with close relations to the Israeli establishment. In 2010, the INSS launched its 'cyber-warfare' research programme led by Dr. Gabi Siboni in cooperation with TAU.[1] In late 2011, Yadlin became the INSS director.

Through the years, the friction over authority in many cyber-related realms has been growing in the IDF. In 2009, the IDF declared cyberspace as an 'operational and strategic war-fighting domain'. The US DoD lifting the self-imposed taboo on speaking about cyber-offense in 2010 probably assisted the IDF statement in 2012, that it's considering offensive cyber-warfare (Katz 2012). The IDF's Operations Directorate recently drafted a document defining the purpose and use of cyber-warfare for the Israeli military. According to the doctrinal document, the IDF views cyberspace as another battlefield parallel to land, sea, or airspace:

> Professionally speaking, the IDF is fighting consistently and relentlessly in cyberspace, is collecting intelligence and protecting the IDF networks as well. When needed, cyberspace is also used to execute attacks and other information operations. (Katz 2012)

The IDF said that the purpose of operations in cyberspace included 'thwarting initiatives by Israel's enemies to undermine the IDF's and Israel's operational freedom' in a wide variety of conflicts (Katz 2012).

Furthermore, following years of overlapping activity, the areas of responsibility in the IDF for cyber-affairs were delineated: the Military Intelligence Unit 8200 received the task of collection and operations while the C4I Corps received cyber-defence, IT-security, and cryptographic foundation tasks. In May 2014, the C4I Corps opened a situational awareness centre to streamline and enhance the IT-security aspect of cybersecurity throughout the defence forces. Contrary to the

[1] Both authors were this program's TAU researchers from 2010 to 2012, working with Dr. Gabi Siboni of the INSS.

sub-unified United States Cyber Command,[2] there is no parallel unified, dedicated cyber-command in the IDF.

Recently (2014), senior IDF officers openly address the topic. Major General Aviv Kochavi, Director of Military Intelligence, says:

> Cyber in my modest opinion will soon be revealed to be the biggest revolution [in warfare], more than gunpowder and the utilisation of air power in the past century.

Kochavi adds that the potential to operate in the cyber-area is almost limitless, but does elaborate further on the issue. The IDF Chief of Staff Lieutenant-General Benny Gantz described cybersecurity as 'vital in the extreme':

> ...[A] playing field that we need to use to the full, and I think that the State of Israel can and should do much more than it has been doing until now [...] must be at the level of a superpower, and it can be at the level of a superpower. (2014)

The possibility to strike high-end protected targets with bits rather than bombs has been demonstrated in reality. Foreign sources often attribute Operation Olympic Games and Operation Orchard to the USA and Israel. While we are not in a position of confirming or denying it, we discuss the above operations conceptually, to elaborate on cyber-warfare role in strategy.

9.2 Cyberattack as a Force Multiplier: Operation Orchard

According to foreign sources, on 6 September 2007 in Operation Orchard, the IAF successfully bombed and destroyed a building complex in Al-Kibar, near the city of Deir ez-Zor in eastern Syria (Dipert 2013; Liff 2012). The secret facility was visible from space, though extensive intelligence efforts were required to establish the purpose of the site. In 2007, the emergent picture was that the building hid the construction of a graphite-cooled nuclear reactor: almost an exact copy of the Yongbyon reactor in North Korea that produces plutonium (Abrams 2013).

The attack on the Syrian reactor project echoes an Israeli raid in 1981 where the IAF destroyed the *Osirak* nuclear reactor in Iraq. But this time, a cyberattack allegedly was central to operational success: overcoming the dense Syrian air defence (Fulghum et al. 2007). According to foreign sources, the extensive Syrian air defence showed no signs of the eight IAF fighter aircrafts in the monitored airspace (Katz and Hendel 2012). Foreign sources assume that this was achieved by a computer intrusion to infiltrate and temporary neutralize the air defence radars and communication systems, so that activity appeared to the operators as normal (Rid 2011, 2013).

---

[2] USCYBERCOM plans, coordinates, integrates, synchronizes, and conducts activities to direct the operations and defense of specified Department of Defense information networks; prepare to, and when directed, conduct full spectrum military cyberspace operations in order to enable actions in all domains, ensure US/Allied freedom of action in cyberspace and deny the same to our adversaries.

Traditionally, such an effect would have required kinetic strikes on the air defence systems' elements. It would necessarily bring the physical destruction of radar installations, possibly killing some of the system's operators, as well as foreign advisors or innocent civilians (Rid 2013).

Operation Orchard demonstrates the blurred line between the more traditional, but no less sophisticated, electronic warfare realm and the newer cyber-warfare capabilities (Fulghum et al. 2007). The clarification of this conceptual issue is beyond the scope of this book. Achieving the desired operational effect with the minimum collateral damage reportedly demonstrated in this case, is in line with the Israeli strategy.

9.3 Operation Olympic Games: Stuxnet as the First Precision-Guided Cyber Weapon

The public disclosure of Stuxnet malware in July 2010 and its subsequent analyses were an eye-opener for the public: it has been by far the most sophisticated known cyberattack to date (Rid 2013; Sanger 2012; Zetter 2014). Stuxnet malware was specifically written to infiltrate and silently disrupt industrial control systems (Singer and Friedman 2014; Farwell and Rohozinski 2011). The malware slowly damaged the centrifuges at Natanz nuclear enrichment facilities in Iran by reprogramming the Siemens programmable logic controller (PLC) that controlled the centrifuges to spin the motor out of the safe range (Langner 2011). To do that, it had to first compromise a Microsoft Windows system, then propagate inside corporate air-gapped networks. The malware probably had been implanted in late 2007; by the end of 2010, the worm had infected approximately 100,000 hosts in dozens of countries, 60 % of which were in Iran (Sanger 2012).

But *infection* does not mean that the *payload* is executed. The malware looked for the Siemens WinCC/PCS 7 supervisory control and data acquisition (SCADA) software on the Windows machine, and continued to identify a specific hardware and software configuration (Denning 2012). It specifically targeted two models of Siemens logic controllers, 6ES7-315-2 and 6ES7-417, and the payload altered the code these PLCs run (Langner 2011). This was accomplished by exploiting several vulnerabilities, one of which was a hardcoded WinCC password (Dipert 2013; Klimburg 2011). If the specific configuration had not been found, the weaponised payload (the PLC code supposedly altering the operation of centrifugal rotation speed) would not have been activated. No damage was done to a system infected that did not meet a precise set of predefined attributes (Rid 2013; Sanger 2012; Zetter 2014). Stuxnet is thus a precision-guided weapon.

Importantly, Stuxnet took over the human–machine interface (HMI) output to display activity as normal and suppress alarms to evade detection (Katz and Hendel 2012). Before Stuxnet started sabotaging ongoing processes, it intercepted input values from sensors—for example, the state of a valve or operating temperatures—recorded these data, and then provided the legitimate controller code with pre-recorded input signals, while the actual processes in the background were manipulated (Langner 2011).

9.3.1 *Stuxnet and Strategic Utility*

What did Stuxnet achieve? The malware likely phisycally destroyed about 1,000 out of the 9,000 IR-1 centrifuges deployed at Natanz in late 2009 and early 2010. The former IAEA Deputy Director General acknowledged that the malware could be 'one of the reasons' for a drop in the number of centrifuges at Natanz, but stated that 'there is no evidence that it was' Moreover, the unexpected rate of failures must have introduced profound insecurity among the members of the nuclear program, the Iranian security apparatus, and the government (Barzashka 2013).

Critics argue that whoever was behind Stuxnet did not succeed in stopping the Iranian regime's determination to develop a nuclear weapon facility (Barzashka 2013; Dipert 2013; Farwell and Rohozinski 2011; Lindsay 2013). One scholar interpreted the findings as such: 'Stuxnet did not considerably set back Iran's nuclear programme and bomb-making potential. If anything, the malware—if it did in fact infiltrate Natanz—has made the Iranians more cautious about protecting their nuclear facilities' (Barzashka 2013). The claims of ineffectiveness do not prevent the same scholar stating that 'using computer malware to attack critical infrastructure sets a dangerous precedent' (Barzashka 2013). While we do not know nearly enough to reach a verdict on Stuxnet strategic value, the operation demonstrates how sophisticated cyber-tools can be employed instead of traditional kinetic attacks, effectively targeting high-value air-gapped targets (Katz and Hendel 2012).

9.4 Discussion: Cyber-Warfare Matures

Eugene Kaspersky passionately warned a 1,500-strong Tel Aviv audience at the June 2012 2nd TAU International Conference that Stuxnet will 'backfire' on Israel and the West (The 2nd Annual Cyber Security International Conference Proceedings 2012). Whether such warnings reached the intended recipients is unknown. However, to rely on a cyberattack in high-risk operations with strategic consequences illustrates the maturity of cyber-warfare achieved by the operators. Sending combat pilots into the killing range of Syrian air defence, while entrusting their safety to a non-kinetic attack, is no less illustrative. Until Stuxnet, the sending of bits to damage physical facilities was only theoretical.

There are several required ingredients for cyber-warfare. The first ingredient is the spectrum of technologies on which it is necessary to gather intelligence, reverse engineer, and infiltrate the target. To target an air defence system or a proprietary air-gapped industrial network is a task clearly more difficult than targeting a standard office. Second, to prefer a cyberattack over alternative operational approaches, the concept must have proven itself and the particular implementation tried and tested. Third, senior stakeholders would need convincing on the validity of the new approach—hardly a trivial task. Therefore, one may assume that considering and using a cyberattack in important operations attests to many years of technological, conceptual, and operational experience.

9.5 Conclusion

The Israeli strategy strives for a qualitative advantage, and has thus emphasised science and technology as the key enabler. Our analysis supports the concept of using cyberspace to achieve qualitative superiority and to develop and employ cyber-arsenal to achieve decisive advantage. Major General Amos Yadlin's 2009 statement that *cyber-warfare suits Israel well* should be taken seriously.

We presented the available public evidence on cyber-warfare in the IDF. The IAF, C4I, and Intelligence branches in particular have pioneered conceptualising, developing, and fielding technical capabilities and human capital for operating in cyberspace. The IDF plays a central role in national cybersecurity capability development, driving much of the Israeli human capital and R&D developments in information technologies, as discussed here and in Chap. 3 above. Two high-profile cyber-operations illustrated the potential of cyber-warfare, as well as the difficulties of damage assessment, effectiveness, attribution, and deterrence. If Israel relied on cyberattacks in such high-risk strategic operations, it attests to the high maturity of technology, doctrine, and organisation of the IDF.

The IDF views cyberspace as a promising realm to achieve decisive operational advantage, yet comprehensive national cybersecurity does not rest solely in the military realm.

References

Abrams E (2013) Tested by Zion: the Bush administration and the Israeli-Palestinian conflict. Cambridge University Press, Cambridge

Baram G (2013) The effect of cyberwar technologies on force buildup: the Israeli case. Mil Strateg Aff 5(1):23–43

Barzashka I (2013) Are cyber-weapons effective? RUSI J 158(2):48–56. doi:10.1080/03071847.2013.787735

Ben-Israel I, Tabansky L (2011) An interdisciplinary look at security challenges in the information age. Mil Strateg Aff 3(3):21–37

Ben-David A (2010) On the offensive. Aviat Week Space Technol 172(13):56–56

Denning DE (2012) Stuxnet: what has changed? Futur Internet 4(3):672–687

Dipert RR (2013) Other-than-internet (OTI) cyberwarfare: challenges for ethics, law, and policy. J Mil Ethics 12(1):34–53

Farwell JP, Rohozinski R (2011) Stuxnet and the future of cyber war. Survival 53(1):23–40

Fulghum DA, Wall R, Butler A (2007) Israel shows electronic prowess. Aviat Week Space Technol 168:25
IDF admits to using cyber space to attack enemies (2012, 06/03/2012) The Jerusalem post
Katz Y (2012) IDF admits to using cyber space to attack enemies. The Jerusalem Post, 06/03/2012. Retrieved from http://www.jpost.com/Defense/IDF-admits-to-using-cyber-space-to-attack-enemies
Katz Y, Hendel Y (2012) Israel vs. Iran: the shadow war. Potomac, Washington, DC
Klimburg A (2011) Mobilising cyber power. Survival 53(1):41–60. doi:10.1080/00396338.2011.555595
Langner R (2011) Stuxnet: dissecting a cyberwarfare weapon. Secur Priv IEEE 9(3):49–51
Liff AP (2012) Cyberwar: a new absolute weapon? The proliferation of cyberwarfare capabilities and interstate war. J Strateg Stud 35(3):401–428
Lindsay JR (2013) Stuxnet and the limits of cyber warfare. Secur Stud 22(3):365–404. doi:10.1080/09636412.2013.816122
Rid T (2011) Cyber war will not take place. J Strateg Stud 35:1–28
Rid T (2013) Cyber war will not take place. Hurst, London
Sanger DE (2012) Confront and conceal: Obama's secret wars and surprising use of American power. Crown, New York
Singer PW, Friedman A (2014) Cybersecurity and cyberwar: what everyone needs to know. Oxford University Press, New York/Oxford
The 2nd Annual Cyber Security International Conference Proceedings (2012) The Yuval Ne'eman workshop for science, technology and security: annual cyber security international conference Tel Aviv
Zetter K (2014) Countdown to zero day: Stuxnet and the launch of the world's first digital weapon. Crown, New York

References

Chapter 10
Conclusion: From Cybersecurity to Cyberpower

Abstract This chapter recapitulates the strategic background and the distinctive phases in the evolution of Israeli cybersecurity policy and cyberpower. The strategic context is essential to comprehend past, present, and future Israeli policy. A general conclusion: While cyberspace is driven by technology, national culture and grand strategy shape cybersecurity policy and practice.

Keywords Cybersecurity • Cyberpower • Innovation ecosystem • Qualitative edge • R&D • National Cyber Initiative • INCB • NCSA • Open society • Israel • Strategy

While information technology enables cyberspace and cyber-risks, non-technical elements such as national culture and grand strategy are crucial in cybersecurity practice, policy, and cyberpower. An analysis of national cybersecurity requires the strategic backdrop. Cybersecurity is not only a matter of acquiring and implementing technical capability. Rather, it is a *policy* issue and, as such, cultural, organisational, and political factors play a crucial role, as our analysis of the Israeli case demonstrates.

> Cybersecurity in Israel is a set of policies and actions with two interconnected goals: mitigating security *risks* and increasing resilience on the one hand, and leveraging *opportunities* enabled by the developing cyberspace on the other hand. We demonstrate how the Israeli grand strategy influences national cybersecurity.

Cyberpower suits the Israeli grand strategy, as it can provide a qualitative edge while not requiring vast natural resources or manpower. Indeed, the IDF plays a central role in national cybersecurity capability development, driving much of the Israeli human capital and R&D developments in information technologies, and overtly views cyberspace as a promising realm to achieve decisive operational advantage. Whoever relies on a cyberattack in high-risk strategic operations, attests to the maturity of their cybersecurity technology, doctrine, and organisation.

L. Tabansky, I. Ben Israel, *Cybersecurity in Israel*, SpringerBriefs in Cybersecurity, DOI 10.1007/978-3-319-18986-4_10

Cyber-warfare may be strategically advantageous for Israel if it proves less deadly and less destructive than kinetic alternatives. However, military capacity is just one element of national cybersecurity. The Israeli cybersecurity posture is the result of continued focus on scientific and technological progress together with human resource development, in accordance with the central principle of the national security concept.

We concisely presented the unique array of historic, cultural, geo-political, economic, organisational and political factors shaping Israeli cybersecurity posture, indigenous capabilities, and policy. This SpringerBrief's focus on the national policy level acknowledges that a multitude of information, security initiatives, standards, and developments in various business sectors stand beyond its scope.

Chapters 2 and 3 provided the essential analytical background on the Israeli grand strategy and the Israeli innovation ecosystem. The central element of *Tfisat HaBitachon*—the grand strategy that Israel has developed to fulfil its vision in a harsh geo-political environment—is the ceaseless quest for a qualitative edge. This grand strategy demands setting goals, shaping and taking actions necessary to achieve them, and mobilising resources—all in an increasingly liberal, democratic, free-market Open Society (Popper 1945, 1687).[1] The Israeli Innovation Ecosystem—the key driver of national security and economy—is a direct manifestation of Israeli grand strategy. Prominent illustrations of the Israeli Innovation Ecosystem are the world's largest gross domestic expenditure on R&D as a share of the GDP,[2] the world's best quality of scientific research institutions, and a highly educated society. Israeli human capital is shaped by the cultural, military, academic, and business experience.

Chapters 4, 5, 6, 7, 8, and 9 presented the distinctive phases and some of the main actors in the evolution of cybersecurity policy in Israel. We discussed the stakeholders' encounters with the inevitable dilemmas and described the policy-making process for improving cybersecurity through acceptable trade-offs between competing values.

Though some elements of the defence and intelligence community have long had leading experience with leveraging cyber technology for their mission, such efforts took definite shape in the Israeli government only in the mid-1990s. Defence leaders, bridging the knowledge gap to civilian branches of government, facilitated cybersecurity efforts, culminating in 2002 with one of the first centralised Critical Infrastructure Protection (CIP) policies in the developed world. The shared responsibility arrangement, where Israel's National Security Authority (NISA) was a professional regulator, proved viable, but as cyberspace developed, so did the risks and opportunities. Cybersecurity for the civilian sector presents all the Open Societies with severe conceptual, political, ethical, legal, and financial challenges;

---

[1] Karl R. Popper defined an Open Society as one in which individuals can question authority. It is not identical to democracy or capitalism, but rather does not punish individuals for expressing criticism.

[2] We assess the share of the defence R&D as *an additional 1–1.5 % of the GDP*, thus bringing the Israeli R&D expenditure close to 6 % of the GDP. See Chap. 3 above.

it is becoming the focus of Israeli policy. In response, the PM tasked Isaac Ben-Israel to lead the 2010 National Cyber Initiative. This external, multi-stakeholder expert review committee pursued a comprehensive approach, looking beyond reducing threat vectors to explore macro-economic and strategic benefits for Israel. The National Cyber Initiative taskforce considered the existing cybersecurity efforts inadequate to the rapidly changing environment. Increased collaboration of government, defence, academia, and industry in the Israeli ecosystem was put forward as the best approach to enhance national cybersecurity and reach the strategic goal of making Israel one of the top-five global cyberpowers. The taskforce report detailed a series of recommendations and since its adoption by the government in 2011 is the basis for the Israeli national cyber-strategy. To develop and implement it, the Prime Minister's office established a new Israeli National Cyber Bureau (INCB). The INCB had promoted significant academic research efforts, export-oriented cyber-industry, professional education, and international cooperation agreements. The national Cyber Event Readiness Team (CERT-IL) will soon begin operation, though the projected outcome of most INCB tasks is too early to assess. The government resolved in February 2015 to establish a new National Cyber Security Authority (NCSA) designed to enhance comprehensive national cybersecurity while reducing the tension between basic freedoms and security. The process includes multiple legislative, organisational, and other efforts expected to last several years. The background and the policy process leading to this change reemphasise the crucial role of non-technical aspects in cybersecurity.

The need for cybersecurity is universal: a rational state would like to promote its domestic and international interests. Undeniably, most states would like to leverage cybersecurity for the citizens and vis-à-vis its opponents. But which states succeed, and why? Strategy and policy are the missing ingredients; this is the subject of this book and the SpringerBriefs in Cybersecurity series. However, the sobering lesson of international history is that although it is usually better to have some kind of strategy than not, unless you are prepared to adapt it as circumstances change, it is unlikely to do you much good (Freedman 2013). This is a humbling perspective on cybersecurity strategy, where one can be seduced by shiny hardware and superior software.

Change is the only constant, now and in the future. This SpringerBrief shares the Israeli experience to enhance fruitful policy efforts in like-minded countries as the developed democracies are in the midst of cybersecurity policy evolution. We hope that Israel and the other Open Societies of the world will leverage their openness to change, dynamism, and flexibility to prosper in the Information Age.

References

Freedman L (2013) Strategy: a history. Oxford University Press, Oxford
Popper KR (1945) The open society and its enemies. G. Routledge & Sons, London

MIX
Papier aus verantwortungsvollen Quellen
Paper from responsible sources
FSC® C105338

If you have any concerns about our products,
you can contact us on
ProductSafety@springernature.com

In case Publisher is established outside the EU,
the EU authorized representative is:
Springer Nature Customer Service Center GmbH
Europaplatz 3, 69115 Heidelberg, Germany

Printed by Libri Plureos GmbH
in Hamburg, Germany